Learning to Predict and Predicting to Learn

Cognitive Strategies and Instructional Routines

Thomas DeVere Wolsey
San Diego State University

Douglas Fisher
San Diego State University

Allyn & Bacon
is an imprint of

PEARSON

Boston   New York   San Francisco
Mexico City   Montreal   Toronto   London   Madrid   Munich   Paris
Hong Kong   Singapore   Tokyo   Cape Town   Syndey

Vice President and Executive Publisher: Jeffery W. Johnston
Senior Editor: Linda Ashe Bishop
Senior Managing Editor: Pamela D. Bennett
Senior Project Manager: Mary M. Irvin
Editorial Assistant: Demetrius Hall
Senior Art Director: Diane C. Lorenzo
Cover Designer: Jeff Vanik
Cover Image: Jupiter Images
Operations Specialist: Matt Ottenweller
Director of Marketing: Quinn Perkson
Marketing Manager: Krista Clark
Marketing Coordinator: Brian Mounts

For related titles and support materials, visit our online catalog at www.ablongman.com

Library of Congress Cataloging-in-Publication Data
Wolsey, Thomas DeVere.
   Learning to predict and predicting to learn : cognitive strategies and instructional
   routines / Thomas DeVere Wolsey, Douglas Fisher.
      p. cm.
   Includes bibliographical references and index.
   ISBN-13: 978-0-13-157922-4 ISBN-10: 0-13-157922-3
   1. Critical thinking—Study and teaching. 2. Reasoning—Study and teaching.
3. Learning strategies. I. Fisher, Douglas, II. Title.
   LB1590.3.W65 2009
   370.15'2—dc22   2007048781

Printed in the United States of America

10 9 8 7 6 5 4 3 2 1   [HAM]   09 08 07 06 05

Acknowledgments

During the course of writing *Learning to Predict and Predicting to Learn*, we depended on our reviewers to provide keen insight and guidance in developing a book that encourages teachers to practice greater precision in lesson planning and teaching. We therefore extend our gratitude to Deanna Birdyshaw, University of Michigan; Jacquelyn Culpepper, Mercer University; James Johnston, Central Connecticut University; Barbara Pettegrew, Otterbein College (Emerita); Debra Price, Sam Houston State University; and Mahmoud Suleiman, California State University–Bakersfield. We thank each of you for your guidance in fine-tuning the cognitive strategies that students can use to improve learning how to predict and the instructional routines that will lead teachers to improve their classroom practices in conveying that knowledge.

Contents

An Introduction to Prediction

Prediction. The word comes to the English language by a circuitous route that began in Rome. The Latin prefix *præ-*, which we know as *pre-*, means "before." It is familiar in the words *prefabricated, prepare, preposition,* and *prewrite. Dicere* seems less familiar, at first; however, the past participle *dictus* can be found in words like *diction, dictionary, dictator,* and *prediction. Dicere* means to speak. A prediction, traced etymologically back to Latin, means something spoken in advance of an event. If you are able to see the connection between the Latin roots and prefixes and the modern English words like *dictation* and *benediction,* then you are familiar with the first principle of good prediction. You looked for and found patterns and associated ideas that at first seemed incompatible. Our brains are wired to do exactly that: make creative and precise predictions based on what we know and the patterns we recognize so we can anticipate what might come next. Our job as teachers is to help students recognize patterns and connect with what they already know to help them become better readers and thinkers.

WHAT IS PREDICTING?

Predicting is a process of refining and thinking with precision. Learning to make, revise, and revisit predictions will provide students with information about how authors write, why they write what they do, and how readers can more meaningfully interact with texts. Teaching students to make predictions and learn from their predictions will ensure that students do, in fact, read and write more and do so better.

So which strategies ensure students become fluent with making prediction? What instructional strategies and teaching approaches help students become proficient at prediction? What evidence-based rationale supports how predicting to learn and learning to predict become critical facets of reading comprehension? These are the questions that this text answers.

❧ PREDICTIONS CREATE PURPOSE

What motivates us to learn, to create, to discover or explore, or to understand, is vital. It is, however, often ignored. Why should students learn that electrons orbit around the nucleus? Obviously, because the teacher says it is important; it is going to be on the test, after all. However, even if teachers are compelled to use extrinsic motivational tools in their teaching practice, the most thoughtful educators know that learning is best when the student wants to learn because the learning itself is interesting. We know students who could not have cared less about their grades, yet were motivated to know the human condition of the greasers in *The Outsiders* (Hinton, 1967); to spend lunch time voluntarily exploring the journey of Lewis, Clark, and the Corps of Discovery; or to understand the complexity of the decision to drop the first nuclear weapon during World War II. The apparent puzzle of students who will not turn in daily work but will spend hours investigating a subject of interest suggests to us that a search for that which is meaningful is far more powerful as a motivator than any score in a grade book. Thinkers look for patterns that are meaningful where otherwise there is great ambiguity. Prediction, as Alfie Kohn (1993) pointed out, can be a powerful means for promoting curiosity, discovery, and engagement.

❧ PREDICTIONS FOR LEARNING

In teaching students to predict, we teach them to become experts. The novice learners of our subject matters and other course content must attend to a great deal of information. Through expert instruction, such novice learners become increasingly familiar with the material. By doing so, some of the episodic (or historical) links may begin to disappear and the rich connections that are worth the learner's attention increase. In prediction, we attend to those features that are most relevant to the problem at hand, bringing to bear an increasing store of relevant information. The novice learners in our classrooms can become experts in the content of our lessons, and they can become experts at learning.

❧ THE STRUCTURE OF THIS BOOK

This text is divided up into four distinct parts. Part I explores why teaching students to predict with precision is an important aspect of reading. We consider various learning theories and information about the way the brain processes and stores information. Part I provides the rationale for sustained focus on predicting as well as the evidence base for defending its use.

In Part II of this book, we turn our attention to the cognitive strategies involved in predicting. These are things that readers do to make and revise predictions. Of course, these strategies can be taught through modeling and discussion. Each of the cognitive strategies in this section is explained and a procedure for teaching students how to use the prediction strategy is laid out. Each strategy closes with authentic classroom examples and artifacts to help you teach the strategy to students.

Part III of this book focuses on instructional strategies—classroom routines—that can be used to facilitate the use of predicting such that students incorporate this type of thinking into their habits. When this occurs, cognitive strategies move to the unconscious control and become skills that the reader automatically uses while reading and thinking. Of course, this is the goal of our instruction—the development of skilled readers who automatically deploy a number of strategies in real time, as they need them.

The final part of this book, Part IV, focuses on routines students can use to learn from the predictions they make. Making predictions is necessary, but learning from predictions (especially predictions that were incorrect) is even more important in developing long-term understanding. In Part IV, we consider the specific use of strategies and routines for specific students, based on what we know about them. As you'll see, learner profiles help us apply the right strategy at the right time, which is part of our definition for teaching with precision.

❧ CONCLUSION

Our experience suggests that predicting is an excellent overarching structure under which a great deal of instruction can be delivered. Learning to predict and learning from predictions is not limited to a specific grade level or content area—predicting is something that has to permeate classroom instruction and interaction. As students are expected to read increasingly difficult texts, they need guidance in using cognitive strategies with unknown vocabulary, complex ideas, and writers who use sophisticated structures and subtle ideas to communicate.

Over time, and with guidance from their teachers, students will incorporate a number of cognitive strategies into their reading repertoires. When they do so, they will read like experts.

REFERENCES

Hinton, S. E. (1967). *The outsiders*. New York: Dell.

Kohn, A. (1993). *Punished by rewards: The trouble with gold stars, incentive plans, A's, praise and other bribes*. Boston: Houghton Mifflin.

1

UNDERSTANDING THE ROLE OF PREDICTING IN LEARNING

Do you know that good readers use predictions all the time—often unconsciously—because it just comes as a natural part of what they have learned to do? Poor readers, however, do not use predictions when they read or do not use them effectively. You can learn, however, to teach all children and adolescents how to predict and how to use prediction as an essential learning strategy. Let's begin by examining how three teachers currently use prediction in their classrooms. As you read each classroom vignette, think about how teachers engage students in predicting and how, if at all, these predictions facilitate students' learning.

 ## *SCENARIO 1: Superficial Predictions and Missed Opportunities*

Thirty-six ninth graders enter their English classroom. They notice the change in the physical environment—there are pictures of the ocean, a large "fish" made of paper, and fishing tackle scattered around the room. One of the windows is covered with paper, and the sea has been drawn on it. The board in the front of the classroom contains a writing prompt: "Write about a struggle you have had with nature." Given their usual routine of bellwork, students open their writer's notebooks and begin writing.

After 15 minutes of writing Ms. James, the teacher, holds up a book and reads the title: *The Old Man and the Sea* by Ernest Hemingway (1952). After a pause, she asks the class, "What do you think this book will be about?" The students look around. Micha raises her hand, "An old guy that goes out to sea?" Javier adds, "Maybe it's about a guy who gets old working out at sea." The class seems to agree and Ms. James continues. She reads the back cover copy about a man who struggles with nature, who finds himself, and who gains a greater understanding of his life. "What do you think now?" she asks the class.

Anthony says, "I guess it's about an old guy who goes out to sea to find himself." Shawntel agrees with Anthony, but says, "This better not be some fishing story like we had last year. I hated that boring story." Ms. James starts to read the first few pages. Several paragraphs into the book, she asks, "Now what do you think?" Shawntel, without raising her hand, says, "See I told y'all—boring."

When she finishes reading aloud, Ms. James asks the class to discuss their predictions for the next section of the story with their peers. Luis quietly says, "I'm not into this book. I think we're gonna have to hear about this old guy's trip."

SCENARIO 2: Using Clues from the Text to Predict

Twenty kindergartners sit on the rug in the front of the room, excitedly waiting for their teacher to start her interactive read-aloud. The students in Ms. Martinez's class know this routine well and appreciate the conversations they have with one another and their teacher during the read-aloud time. Ms. Martinez uncovers the book, which was sitting on the easel under a sheet of paper. "*Ten Dogs in the Window*," (Masurel, 1997) she says. "Let's see, do we all remember our numbers? Let's count the number of dogs in the window to see if we agree with the author. Are there really ten dogs in the window?" Together the students count as Ms. Martinez points to each dog. "Yes, ten dogs. I wonder why they are in that window. It's a very nice window. Let's see. I think they all belong to one family and they are waiting for their family to come home. What do you think? Why are they in the window? Angel?"

Angel responds, "My dog likes to wait in the window. I only got one dog."

Ms. Martinez listens to Angel and says, "Maybe that's what the author is going to tell us about—dogs waiting in the window for their people to come home. But room nine, we know that we're not always right with our predictions the first time. Why else would those ten dogs be in the window? Creshena?"

Creshena looks up at her teacher and says, "They at the pound. That place, you know, where you could get a new dog." Quefon raises his hand, "Maybe they be lookin' for a new house; new people?" Ms. Martinez pauses and says, "Interesting. I just don't know. We have some good predictions. Partner A, please tell your partner why you think those ten dogs are in the window." At this point, the classroom fills with talk. Students are sharing predictions with one another.

Ms. Martinez says, "Okay room nine. Remember those predictions. Let's see what the author has to tell us." She then begins reading the book. Several pages into the book Ms. Martinez says, "So, the dogs are looking for new places to live. Did you notice how each person who picks out a dog looks like the dog he or she picks? Let's look at this person—he's wearing a red jacket and hat. He has a big moustache. Which dog do you predict he'll want to take home?" The class agrees that the Scottish terrier will be picked next, and sure enough the students get it right. Ms. Martinez says, "Let's look back at that page. How did you know? What clues did the author or illustrator give you that this man might pick this dog? Talk with your partners." Around the room, children talk about the look of the dog, the look of the man, the fact that both have "whiskers" on their face, and that in the illustration the dog is one of two dogs looking toward the man. Ms. Martinez continues reading the book, allowing students to predict which person will adopt which dog. Each time they do so, she flips back a page and asks students how they made their predictions.

SCENARIO 3: Incorporating Prior Knowledge into Predictions

"Okay, what do we know so far?" asks Mr. Jackson of his sixth-grade social science class. "Yes, Jessica, tell us something."

"Well, Greece is a great place. They created a country that other people envied." Jessica reports to the class.

"The art, the politics, the architecture, they had everything. Other groups had tried to conquer them, but they always won. They were the best of the best!" adds Brian.

"So, will Macedonia attack Greece?" asks Mr. Jackson. "Using what you know so far, do you think this small country will attack the 'best of the best' as Brian put it? Write your predictions in your history journals—let's take three minutes. Ready?"

After three minutes of independent writing, Mr. Jackson starts reading from the text:

> Macedonia lay north of Greece. The Macedonians raised sheep and horses and grew crops in their river valleys. They were a warrior people who fought on horseback. The Greeks looked down on them, but by 400 B.C., Macedonia had become a powerful kingdom. (Spielvogel, 2006, p. 399)

"Let's talk about this. The author seems to provide support for both sides of the issue. Have any of you changed your minds or are your predictions still holding?" asks Mr. Jackson.

"I've changed a bit," says Dominique. "I originally wrote that Macedonia wouldn't be so stupid as to attack powerful Greece. After hearing that, I think they will attack, but that they'll lose. They fight on horses, but Greece is so powerful and has so many people."

"I didn't change my prediction," notes Kaila. "Greece isn't a big deal now, so they had to lose at some time."

"Let's see if you're right," Mr. Jackson says and continues reading:

> In 359 B.C., Philip II rose to the throne in Macedonia. Philip had lived in Greece as a young man. He admired everything about the Greeks—their art, their ideas, and their armies. Although Macedonia was influenced by Greek ideas, Philip wanted to make his kingdom strong enough to defeat the mighty Persian Empire. In order to achieve this goal, Philip needed to unite the Greek city-states with his own kingdom. (Spielvogel, 2006, p. 399)

"Okay, so this guy Philip wants to make this happen. It seems pretty clear that he's going to make a try for Greece. Now the author has given you his strategy. He needs to unite the city-states. What do you need to know to make a good prediction about the outcome of this strategy?" asks Mr. Jackson.

Jeff says, "Well, you gotta know what a city-state is and you have to know about Greece and Macedonia."

Gabby adds, "You gotta use everything you know AND what the author is telling you. He said that the new king was named Philip. So, I remember Philip the Great. His name tells me something. I also know that Greece loses power. Their government was organized into city-states, which has both good points and bad points. The author also said that

Philip lived in Greece, so I think he knows how to get at the city-states. I think his strategy will work and he'll be the ruler of all of the land."

Having glimpsed the instruction in three different classrooms, what are your thoughts about the usefulness of making predictions as a learning strategy? Did you notice that predictions were not used equally in each of the three classrooms we visited?

In the first classroom, Ms. James missed a number of opportunities to model and teach predictions. The students probably wondered why their classroom environment had changed and why all of the sea life cluttered the room. Simply using the book title and back cover copy did not result in sophisticated predictions or increased interest or engagement in the text. In this classroom, a good idea—helping students make predictions—was not implemented in a way that helped students learn.

In the second classroom, Ms. Martinez taught her kindergartners to pay close attention to the text to make, confirm, and revise their predictions. The students in this classroom benefited from classroom talk, teacher modeling, and purposeful instruction that served to focus their attention. With practice, the students in this classroom are likely to learn how to use features in the text—both the author's words and the illustrator's ideas—to understand what they read.

In the third classroom, Mr. Jackson activated his students' background and prior knowledge and helped his students make connections between what they know and what they are reading. These students are engaged in authentic interactions and transactions with the text as they learn to negotiate meaning (e.g., Rosenblatt, 1995). Mr. Jackson clearly communicates the idea that answers are not simply found in the text or that the text has one right interpretation. Instead, he is teaching his students that reading is a complex interaction between cognitive engagement, textual understanding, and stored knowledge.

From these scenarios, at least three reasons for creating and maintaining a focus on teaching students to make predictions are evident: engagement, activating background knowledge, and exercising the use of reading strategies.

❦ THE BENEFITS OF MAKING PREDICTIONS

Engagement

Engagement is a major goal all teachers have for their students. To be engaged in reading, to want to read to understand, is directly linked with learning (Frey, 2004; Guthrie & Wigfield, 1997). In other words, it's hard to learn in the absence of engagement.

When students make predictions in an authentic way, they are more engaged in reading, talking, writing, listening, and learning. Making predictions requires that the learner is paying attention to the task at hand. Making predictions also encourages students to talk with one another and with their teacher—which is another way to increase engagement.

As you no doubt noticed from Ms. Martinez's and Mr. Jackson's classrooms, students were engaged in the lesson. They were paying attention, and their brains were focused on the text and what they wanted to know about it. In both cases, student learning increased because of this engagement.

Activating Existing Knowledge

In making a prediction, students use what they already know to inform their supposition of what might happen next. Making a prediction requires that students think about what they already know, what their life experiences have taught them, and how the world works. Beyond engagement, activating and building background knowledge is directly linked with student achievement (Marzano, 2004).

The best example of activating background knowledge we have presented thus far occurred in Mr. Jackson's classroom. He regularly asked students to incorporate what they already knew—from personal experience or formal schooling—into their responses. In doing so, Mr. Jackson facilitated his students' transactions with the text and developed their schema for understanding the world.

Exercising the Use of Reading Strategies

When students make predictions at the onset of their reading or as they engage in reading, they will benefit from using a wide variety of reading skills and strategies beyond "predictions." Of course, predicting requires the integration of a number of cognitive strategies, such as visualizing, inferring, summarizing, and connecting. With practice, students will begin making predictions and using strategies with increased automaticity and ease.

Of course, using reading strategies in authentic and automatic ways improves students' achievement (Fisher & Frey, 2004). Not all students are aware of all the strategies available to them to improve their ability to make reading predictions. However, teachers can provide students with a wide repertoire of strategies that can help them self-regulate their own reading. In this way, they become better predictors and thus skilled readers.

In the class scenarios in this section, students engaged in text clues, inferring, summarizing, and making connections. Ms. Martinez, for example, helped students use visual clues and specific words in making predictions. Mr. Jackson focused on connections and summarizing as his students made predictions. These teachers helped their students make predictions based on reading.

Making predictions is not new. Humans have used their skills in predicting for centuries. Predicting, at least at the human race level, can even be considered a survival skill.

✿ HUMANS: A HISTORY OF PREDICTING

The ability to use cognitive talent in predicting what might happen next is one way humans have learned to survive as a species. Nomadic tribes, for example, use prediction as a way of life. As they travel from place to place, members of the tribe predict where they might find herds of game, where they might find sources of water, where potential enemies might be hiding out, or where friends and trading partners might be located.

For about 11,000 years, many cultures have produced food and relied on prediction to ensure a stable food supply. To be a farmer is to be a prognosticator. Will there be a drought this year or next? How much land can I cultivate if I hire ten people to work for me this year? What will be the long-term effect if I continue to use certain herbicides or pesticides on my farm?

Jared Diamond (1999) proposed that successful domestication of plants and animals led to food storage and surpluses which, when coupled with many other factors, led to some cultures becoming technologically more advanced. Without predictive abilities, Diamond contends, food production on such a scale would not have been possible and the technology we now find commonplace might not yet exist. In other words, our ability to predict resulted in the advancement of society.

Predictions Reduce Uncertainty

Predictions are the means we use to reduce those elements of our world about which we are uncertain. The way we do that is to continually aggregate or collect information and compare that against other knowledge we have stored away. Without stored information and the ability to gather new information, predictions are little more than wild guesses. Such guesses are useless in making sense of an environment upon which we depend for survival and for meaning. Predictions allow people to examine their past and present situations to make meaningful new estimations about what the future might hold.

Given the importance of human predictive ability, we can ask ourselves how the brain makes sense of the world in order to make predictions. Bound up in the capacity to make predictions are theories of memory, learning, and recall—elements that allow for receiving, storing, and retrieving information, which are critical components in making predictions.

✺ PROCESSING INFORMATION: A CRITICAL ASPECT OF PREDICTION

A model for processing information—or learning, cognition, and memory—is found in Figure I.1. In this model, based on the work of Frank Smith (2004), working memory and

Figure I.1   A Model of Information Processing

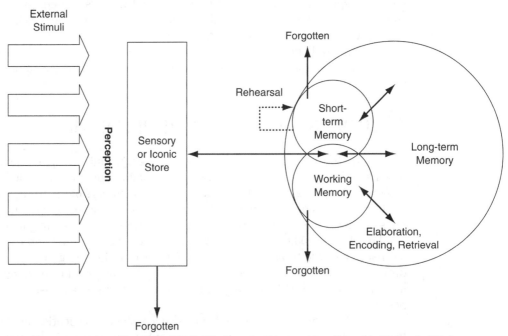

Source: Adapted from Smith, F. (2004). *Understanding reading* (6th ed.). Mahwah, NJ: Lawrence Erlbaum Associates.

short-term memory appear as two different, but overlapping, memory systems. The distinction is important in describing how the brain processes information that could result in a prediction.

Short-Term Memory

Short-term memory is very limited in its capacity for storage. New information can push other information aside. For example, have you ever tried to remember a phone number being told to you only to realize that you forgot why you were calling? In short-term memory, information must be used quickly or it will be forgotten.

Short-term memory is too limited in the amount of information it can store and in the length of time before memory decays without rehearsal to complete complex cognitive functions. In other words, short-term memory has limited use in making predictions. We cannot make predictions about the meaning of a complex sentence unless we are able to store sufficient information about individual words while also reading ahead to determine which other words might change the meaning of the sentence as a whole.

Try an example. Read the sentence fragment below and focus on the word *running*.

I am running. . .

At this point in the sentence, you have some idea that you (as the first-person "I") have become the subject of the verb, and you know that the verb is *running*. However, you do not yet know what other contexts will appear to help you determine exactly what *running* means. You will have to read the rest of the sentence to get that information, all the time retaining the possible meanings for the word until you can reduce the uncertainty you have about the eventual meaning of the sentence. If the meaning is that you have an errand to attend to quickly, then the sentence could be:

I am running to the store to buy milk and eggs.

But if the meaning is that you will have to propel yourself very quickly on foot, then the sentence could be:

I am running a marathon tomorrow at noon.

The final determination of the meaning of the word—and thus of the sentence—has to be stored and integrated as the rest of the sentence is read, possibly with preceding sentences or those that might follow.

"Do you have the results of the test?" asked Maria?

"I am running the analysis software, right now," replied Bill.

Ah, now you know that *running*, in this case, refers to executing or processing information on a computer. To make sense of the final sentence, you needed to pull your knowledge about computers forward from long-term memory into working memory.

Working Memory: Pulling Stored Knowledge Forward

Working memory allows the thinker to bring long-term memory forward along with information stored in short-term memory until such time as

- the problem is solved,
- the information is integrated, or
- the effort is abandoned.

Working memory, described by Baddeley (2001), is a means of temporarily storing and maintaining information during complex cognitive processes. This is particularly relevant to our discussion of predictions and how they are made because, in predicting, the thinker brings forward relevant information from long-term memory and integrates it with any new information already in working memory, applying it to the problem at hand. As you remember from the class discussion Mr. Jackson facilitated, Kaila used her working memory (that "Greece isn't a big deal now") to shape her thinking about the text she was reading and the discussion she was having with others.

Long-Term Memory and Prior Knowledge

Memories that the thinker has stored for later retrieval may be thought of as long-term. When you remember your first-grade teacher, the smell of a favorite aunt's perfume, the structure of the Bohr atom, or the birthdays of your friends, you are using long-term memory. Memories that are stored in a long-term memory reservoir have been characterized in various ways by different researchers. They have been referenced as schemata (Bartlett, 1932), prior knowledge, nonvisual information (Smith, 2004), cognitive structure, and learning (Dechant, 1991). Regardless of the label, a common feature of long-term memory is that it changes the structure of neurons. These changes occur through a process of rehearsal and meaningful association between what is already known and the new information being considered. Of course, long-term memory is not always permanent; we all have experience with the natural forgetting process associated with long-term memory.

Arrangement or organization is the basis of long-term memory. How we organize information is at least as important as the information itself. Without storing information in a particular order or hierarchical structure, the retrieval of relevant information would not be possible.

Types of Long-Term Memory   Theories of long-term memory suggest that humans use classification systems to aid their memory. In these systems, the capability of using memory to organize ideas roughly follows evolutionary lines. Humans use three types of long-term memory for survival. In addition, humans use three types of long-term memory for learning. Let's consider each of these types and how they relate to learning experiences.

Procedural memories—the use of objects or movements of the body—are the most ancient form of memory and the type as we share with animals. Organisms that rely solely on procedural memory respond to external stimuli and adapt to the environment accordingly. In school, we use procedural memories to move around, to multiply numbers, to write, and so on. Procedural memory is critical to the basic functioning of a living organism.

Nested inside our procedural memory is something called semantic memory. Semantic memory permits a person to visualize that which is not actually present at the time. Tulving (1985) suggested that semantic memory allows the thinker to construct and manipulate "mental models" (p. 387) of the world.

You can, for example, create a mental model of a pencil and what it's used for, even when the object is not right in front of you. Semantic memory also allows us to create mental models of ideas. Although your mental model of summer vacation may be different than the model created by those around you, we can discuss our shared understanding of summer vacations with one another. We can think of semantic memory as the type that allows the thinker to manage and relate memory purposefully.

The third type of memory, episodic, permits a thinker to consider events personally experienced in the past, including the emotions of the experience. Among other things, episodic memory makes it possible for the thinker to recall the past and to use that information in constructing an understanding of the present. Consider, for example, the student who has had wonderful experiences at school interacting with teachers. These episodic memories help the student construct his or her participation in the class. Similarly, readers use episodic memories as they read. For example, recalling fresh snow and the emotions of that experience can help a reader let's preserve the notion of activating memories understand how a specific character in a specific book facing a similar experience might react. In other words, episodic memory influences our background knowledge.

We can see the usefulness of this model if we take into account the examples from the beginning of this book and this section. As you read about words that shared the same Latin root as *prediction*, you were able to employ semantic memory to associate words and to see the associations between the words we suggested. When you read the opening paragraphs of the introduction, you probably thought of various predictions you made recently, which demonstrated your episodic memory. You might have remembered the last time the football team played at home, and that the traffic was terrible. This caused you to predict that the traffic might creep along again today because there is a game. Finally, we should clarify that teachers and linguists often think of semantics in terms of words and their meaningful relations in sentences. Here, the term takes on a much broader meaning that includes more than just the meanings of words. Semantic memory also includes an understanding of the function of the idea the word names.

Schemata and Knowledge   As we have discussed, several theories or models of long-term memory exist. Each explains aspects of how we clarify, order, and store representations of the world as we perceive it. Memory is such a complex aspect of being human that no single theory can, at present, fully account for it. Therefore, it isn't necessary to think of one theory as being correct, or even more correct, than another. Taken together, we build an increasingly accurate understanding of how memory works and what aspects of memory make us uniquely human. One other theory of memory that makes us uniquely human is how we "build schema" to order information we take into our long-term memories.

A schema (Bartlett, 1932) is a hierarchical representation of knowledge; in other words, a plan for memories. The theory explains how long-term memory traces might be structured so that memories might be retrieved as they are needed. Here is how it might work.

Prediction depends on existing knowledge   Imagine that a researcher leads you blindfolded into a classroom after school. The teacher and students are gone. The blindfold is removed and your only task is to determine if the class that meets in the room is a primary or upper elementary grade, a middle school grade, or a high school grade. In just an instant, you would be able to give a fairly accurate assessment of the grade level. You could do this without reading anything that might indicate what the grade level is because the size of the desks and chairs and other room paraphernalia would indicate that the room was designed for a specific age group of children.

To visualize a first-grade classroom, you need to recognize what you observed as elements of a first-grade room (small desks, big books, etc.), visually sample the rest, and draw your conclusion based on the map or plan you have in your memory for this concept. Organization of the memory traces associated with this concept makes it possible to retrieve all the elements in a search for the overall pattern.

If the first-grade classroom is somewhat familiar to you, then we can draw one of two conclusions. You went to the same first-grade classroom that the book's authors attended, or more likely, your first-grade classroom looks a lot like ours. A learning theorist would term the degree of accuracy of the mental model to the reality of the concept as veridical. This concept is important and goes back to our earlier discussion about reducing uncertainty. Increasing veridicality means reduced uncertainty.

It may help you to construct this new schema for *veridical* by thinking of other similar concepts. As you read the word, notice that the first three letters are the same as in the word *very*; in fact, the *y* and *i* may have similar roots in the way the words are pronounced. Your schema for *very* tells you that it is an adjective or adverb that is used when a speaker or writer wants to emphasize the precision or truth of whatever the topic happens to be. This reminds you that the coat of arms for Harvard University has the word *veritas* on it. Even if you didn't attend Harvard, you may remember that it has something to do with truth and that it is Latin. Simultaneously, you think of the word *veracity* which you read in this morning's paper in an article about a reporter checking to make sure his source told an accurate story. If you are an English major, you might even remember the word *verisimilitude*, which describes a quality of good fiction that appears to represent a truth about the condition of being human.

In this process, you are activating several existing schemata for words that share the same root and making predictions about what the word might mean. Of course, readers don't limit their use of schemata to words. As Louise Rosenblatt (1978, 1995) noted, readers construct meaning from text through a transactional process. She believed that what the reader brought to the text was at least as important as what the author may have intended.

Predictions depend on actively transforming knowledge   We can say that without schemata that already exist in the mind of the reader/thinker, reading would not be possible. Nevertheless, readers cannot rely solely on their own existing concepts and experiences when attempting to comprehend a text. Communication would be severely restricted if they did so (Dechant, 1991). Rather, readers must build on what they know and transform it as they read or engage in other ways with the world around them. As readers, we know how to make sense of difficult sentence structures, determine how the author organizes the text or story, or look for clues that might foreshadow future events in a narrative. It's just that we don't necessarily think consciously about doing it, although we are able to do so indirectly. In this way, just as you did by examining words that contain the Latin *ver*, you were able to construct an increasingly veridical understanding of that term. As you increasingly bring appropriate schemata to bear and gather new information from reading, you reduce uncertainty by making predictions about the word.

The key, then, becomes teaching our students to be more precise in how they predict by making more efficient use of their knowledge or memory. Predicting is a cognitive procedure that is built on both declarative and procedural knowledge. While it is common for people to predict the uncertain nature of their world, doing so with precision can be taught—precision that will allow students to become experts at predicting.

❧ DEVELOPING EXPERT PREDICTORS

Think for a moment what it means to be an expert at something. What is it that could be described as "expertness?" Expertness requires sophisticated uses of memory. Experts have to mobilize information so they have the right information for the situation at hand.

Analogies Help Us Predict

Analogies are tools that help us become experts at learning how to predict. Let's explore a concrete example to see how.

In the late eighteenth century, Robert Burns was collecting songs and writing poems in Scotland. Many of those songs and poems are still well known today. One poem, also written as a song, is "A Red, Red Rose." The opening lines are immediately recognizable for a famous simile they contain:

O My luve's like a red, red rose,

That's newly sprung in June.

In this analogy, readers quickly realize that Burns' love does not have petals or a long stem. In fact, that thought probably does not even occur as we read the poem. Immediately, readers begin mapping the similarities between roses and the ones they love (or the condition of being in love). The reader may be thinking:

- Love is beautiful, just as a rose is
- Love is sweet, like the fragrance of a rose
- Love is delicate and elegant just like a rose
- Love is new, like a newly blossomed rose and its "newness" is what makes it delicate like a rose, fragile as of yet

For some readers, these would be relatively shallow comparisons or similarities. Readers can also compare what they know about roses as they renew themselves every spring. Thus, love also renews itself and always remains fresh.

In constructing an analogy, the brain first constructs an initial search for similarities between the source and the target analog (the components of the analogy). One way to think about this is to think of the source analog as an already existing schema or as background knowledge. The target analog is the concept or schema that begs to be understood. Once an initial partial map of similarities is made, then the thinker may look for more detailed similarities or extensions of the initial partial mapping.

An interesting series of experiments reported by Holyoak and Thagard (1995) described how a chimpanzee named Sarah learned to make analogies. Sarah was taught to use a series of plastic tokens to represent ideas (or propositions). She learned to use tokens for the concepts of "same" and "different" as well. Many animals can pick out or match items that are the same in physical nature, but Sarah learned to do something far more interesting. She could identify what the relations were between objects that were not the same in physical appearance. For example, Sarah could correctly match objects that were smaller than or larger than a target object even if the physical shape was different. In one experiment, she correctly matched a source analog of a glass half-filled with water to a target analog when given the option of a half of an apple or three-fourths of an apple by correctly choosing the half apple. There is no reason to match a fraction of an apple with a glass of water based solely on physical properties. Sarah had to determine the relation of the glass of water and the apple based on the relation of concepts that are implicit.

Sarah's accomplishments are remarkable for a couple of reasons. One is that Sarah was able to learn something based on the symbolic manipulation of ideas. Another is that such learning was the direct result of her ability to use symbols, an ability she was taught and which other chimps lack, to create abstractions that identify implicit relations between objects. Such implicit relations are the type of thinking that allows humans to compare a rose with one's love. While Sarah used tokens to communicate in a language-like manner, people are much more adept at manipulating symbols. Of course, the symbol system readers most often use is language.

Analogies Clarify Understanding   Analogies help us refine and connect knowledge that we might not have been able to connect otherwise. Gick and Holyoak (1983) have studied analogies extensively and explain their functions: "The analogist notes correspondences between the known problem and a new unsolved one, and on that basis derives an analogous potential solution. More generally, the function of an analogy is to derive a new solution, hypothesis, or prediction..." (p. 5).

In creating analogies, the thinker must notice that there is a similarity that might prove useful. Then, through a process of abstraction, the thinker completely maps the similarities, which cognitive scientists call identities. The differences are also noted. The possibility of mapping every aspect of a source analog onto the target analog is very small, so identification of differences which are not helpful may also be important. If readers continue thinking about Burns' rose, they might also think that their rose, like their love, is beautiful, elegant, and always fresh. Some readers might then think that roses also have thorns and our love also has... Hmmm, better not finish that analogy unless we want to spend the next week or so sleeping on the couch ... or in the doghouse.

Analogies Help Us Predict with Greater Detail   As noted, analogies can help us understand predictions. An incomplete, partial map of an analogy requires predictive ability to continue abstracting the rest of the map. However, a mapped analogy—one that provides a link between the source and the target ideas—may be useful in constructing additional analogies with greater detail. We may want to explore, for example, the analogy that human cognition is like the operation of a computer. Initially, we find that there are several identities or similarities that are useful and map them this way (see Table I.1).

With this initial mapping, we can predict that humans might be overshadowed by computers at some point in the future. However, we also find that there are several differences. If these differences are not relevant to the problem we are trying to solve or

Table I.1   Considering the Analogy between Humans and Computers

Computers	Humans	Similarities
The random access memory (RAM) in a computer is like	Short-term and working memory	Each stores information for temporary processing until it is pushed aside by other information or is no longer needed.
The hard drive is like	Long-term memory	Each stores information indefinitely.
The modern computer's processor is very fast	The human brain is very fast	Each processes information through distributed and parallel processes

the concept we are trying to understand, then the analogy still works. If not, then we will have to abandon the analogy. As we construct this analogy, we remember what David Norman (1997) wrote about humans and computers. He compared humans and computers by addressing the fear that computers will eventually surpass human abilities. Computers, he says, do not present a threat to humans because there are inherent differences in how human systems and computer systems operate. Computers can produce repeatable and accurate results, but humans follow "a complex-history-dependent mode of operation and yield approximate, variable results" (p. 29). Computers do not handle errors very well, but human systems are adaptable to a changing environment and conditions.

Norman's comparison of computers and humans helps us understand a bit about why people are so good at making predictions and why we have come to rely on our predictive skills. Predictions are the means we use to reduce those elements of our world about which we are uncertain. The way we do that is to continually aggregate or collect information and compare that against other knowledge we have stored away. Without stored information and the ability to gather new information, predictions are little more than wild guesses. Such guesses are useless in making sense of an environment upon which we depend for survival and for meaning. Predictions allow people to examine their past and present situations to make meaningful new estimations about what the future might hold. Let's continue and find some differences:

- Computers handle calculations based on precise algorithms that do not tolerate error.
- Humans seek patterns and process information in spite of errors and ambiguity.

Based on this analogy, we can then use the information comparing humans and computers to predict that computers will not surpass human abilities.

Analogies Provide a Bridge to New Learning   In their experiments with analogies and how people use them, Gick and Holyoak (1983) conducted an instructive experiment. They had participants in the experiment read a story that identified a specific solution to a problem. Next they had those participants read a story that presented a similar problem, but did not provide the solution. The first story presented a military situation. A general must attack a fortress in the center of enemy territory. He can't mount a frontal assault with a large force because the roads leading to the fortress are mined. A large force would not be able to move quickly through the minefield. A solution is to send small groups of soldiers to attack by coming at the fort through the minefields from several directions.

In the next story, the subject will encounter a different domain. Instead of a military problem, it might be a medical problem. In this scenario, a tumor must be removed; however, the dose of radiation needed to kill the tumor will also destroy the surrounding tissue. The subjects are then asked to solve the problem.

Because the source analog (the fortress) was in a different domain (the military) than the tumor problem (medical), Gick and Holyoak found something interesting that is useful for teachers. Their participants were successful 75% of the time in mapping the military source analog with the medical target analog to solve the problem. The means for removing the tumor was to target the radiation from several directions so that the surrounding tissue did not receive a lethal dose of radiation but the tumor did. In each analog, the solution lies in coming at the object of the attack (either with soldiers or radiation) from varying directions. However, Gick and Holyoak were able to achieve the 75% rate of correct solutions only when the participants were given a hint. That is, they were told that the military problem could be used to solve the medical problem. Then it was up to the participants to correctly map the two different domains to solve the problem.

This experiment and the resulting conclusions suggest to us as teachers that we need to provide direction, or hints and clues, to help students scaffold their specific predictions about texts they read. We believe that such hints help students learn to construct reasonable and meaningful predictions in specific situations, and also that this type of help assists students in learning to predict and create other types of analogies as part of a process of making meaning of the challenging texts they read.

Comparison Activities as an Expert Skill

Teachers of English language arts often use Venn diagrams to help students compare information from the books they read. Indeed, Marzano, Pickering, and Pollock (2001), in their meta-analysis of effective classroom strategies, found that comparison activities produce the highest effect size of all the strategies studied in increasing student achievement. These researchers identified four important points regarding instruction that makes use of classification based on similarities and comparisons. They are:

1. Present students with explicit guidance in identifying similarities and differences.
2. Ask students to independently identify similarities and differences.
3. Represent similarities and differences in graphic or symbolic form.
4. Identify similarities and differences in a variety of other ways. Such practice helps learners develop a repertoire of approaches and reinforces the use of the cognitive strategy (p. 20).

As these researchers noted, the identification of similarities and differences is a highly robust activity and one that leads to increased student achievement. Making effective predictions involves the use of making comparisons of similar patterns of events, situations, personalities, and geographic locations against new information in order to make an inference about what may happen. To do so with precision and creativity reduces uncertainty on a journey across country, in a movie or novel, and in one's journey through life.

Is Making Predictions Enough?

The simple answer is no. Even as students are taught all of the skills required to make predictions, simply making a prediction will likely not be sufficient for students to think deeply about text. Instead, as teachers, we need to extend the making of predictions to helping students learn from their predictions. For example, Ms. Martinez ensured that her students revisit their predictions and develop a strong sense of which predictions worked and why. She also asked them to figure out what they missed when their predictions were not confirmed. This critical analysis of predictions can improve student learning.

Similarly, illustrated through Ms. James's classroom, asking students to make predictions when there isn't really anything to predict or when the question in focus has been answered in an obvious way will not help students learn. Re-focusing student predictions in Ms. James's class might have changed the nature and depth of the classroom discussions about *The Old Man and the Sea* and created a more motivating reason for students to read the text and begin to understand its value for readers.

✿ LEARNING FROM PREDICTIONS: I PREDICT . . . NOW WHAT?

Part II explains several cognitive strategies that students might use to make good predictions. Part III then puts these cognitive strategies in context of the classroom structures teachers might use to promote better thinking through predictions. Finally, Part IV provides an analysis of which students need which types of instruction to be successful.

We also highlight the idea that readers can learn from predictions. You might say, "Readers learn by making increasingly accurate predictions as they read, learn new information, put that in context of their existing knowledge, and move ahead to see what else there is to learn in the text. Students learn from prediction by making the predictions in the first place." And you are right, but there's more. There are at least two reasons:

1. Readers make predictions because doing so brings relevant existing knowledge to bear as the reader makes meaning.
2. Readers learn from prediction by applying what they know about the text as they read, reducing uncertainty about the content, whether it is primarily aesthetic or efferent in nature (Rosenblatt, 1995), as they go.

Teachers are in the unique position of guiding students' reading, through continuous feedback, direct instruction, modeling, and so on. Through these processes, teachers point out to students what good readers do and assist students to become expert readers. More specifically, through scaffolding or a helping interaction, teachers can assist students to learn what aspects of a text need their attention. Children are less likely to efficiently regulate attention (Berninger & Richards, 2002) and, as a result, require more guidance. The significance for teachers is that it is simply not enough to ask students to make predictions. Instead, teachers must actively show students what needs their attention and how to access that through the cognitive processes explored in Part II and promote their use through practice and classroom structures or routines like those in Part III. Teachers must also help students learn to attend to the predicting process itself. An example may help.

A popular (but fictional) television personality, Chef Lecteur, has just shown his adoring viewers how to make New England clam chowder. At the beginning, he predicted that a few pinches of salt and few grinds of the pepper mill will suffice. However, in the process of making the chowder, variables crept in: the potatoes weren't as fresh because they've been in storage, the onions had a slightly stronger flavor than usual, and so on. A viewer might predict that Lecteur was following a recipe that will turn out a delicious soup if the correct ingredients in the correct amounts were assembled. Just as Lecteur is ready to serve the chowder, he dips a spoon into the pots, blows on the soup in the bowl of the spoon, and tries it. Wait! He reaches for the pepper mill again. Didn't he get it right the first time? He's an expert, and his name is on products that fill his fans' kitchens. As he tastes the soup, he points out how important it is to re-season the food prior to serving: the taste may change through the cooking process. The variables have changed the taste and could not be predicted precisely. What is more important, and what his fans admire, is that he tells them what he did and why he did it. In this way, reading is like cooking because the good cook reassesses the taste of the food right up until it's time to serve the food; the reader re-evaluates predictions right up until the cover of the book is closed. Teachers live for the moments when the metaphorical light bulb comes on for students; Lecteur's fans clap and cheer when he grabs the pepper mill. Like our make-believe chef's fans, students will smile and the lights will illuminate on their faces when they understand why revisiting an earlier prediction creates a more meaningful reading experience. They get it. In Part II we examined the role of cognitive strategies students use to make meaning and predict their way through text. In Part III, instructional routines are presented that teachers use to promote precision as students learn to make predictions that help them learn.

REFERENCES

Baddeley, A. D. (2001). Is working memory still working? *American Psychologist, 56,* 849–864.

Bartlett, F. C. (1932). *Remembering: A study in experimental and social psychology.* Cambridge: Cambridge University Press.

Berninger, V. W., & Richards, T. C. (2002). Brain literacy for educators and psychologists. San Diego: Academic Press.

Dechant, E. (1991). *Understanding and teaching reading: An interactive model.* Hillsdale, NJ: Lawrence Erlbaum Associates.

Diamond, J. (1999). *Guns, germs, and steel: The fates of human societies.* New York: W. W. Norton and Company.

Fisher, D., & Frey, N. (2004). *Improving adolescent literacy: Strategies at work.* Upper Saddle River, NJ: Merrill Prentice Hall.

Frey, N. (2004). *The effective teacher's guide: 50 ways for engaging students in learning.* San Diego, CA: Academic Professional Development.

Gick, M. L., & Holyoak, K. J. (1983). Schema induction and analogical transfer. *Cognitive Psychology, 15,* 1–38.

Guthrie, J. T., & Wigfield, A. (Eds.). (1997). *Reading engagement: Motivating readers through integrated instruction.* Newark, DE: International Reading Association.

Hemingway, E. (1952). *The old man and the sea.* London: Jonathan Cape.

Holyoak, K. J., & Thagard, P. (1995). *Mental leaps: Analogy in creative thought.* Cambridge, MA: The MIT Press.

Marzano, R. J. (2004). *Building background knowledge for academic achievement.* Alexandria, VA: Association for Supervision and Curriculum Development.

Marzano, R. J., Pickering, D. J., & Pollock, J. (2001). *Classroom instruction that works: Research-based strategies for increasing student achievement.* Alexandria, VA: Association for Supervision and Curriculum Development.

Masurel, C. (1997). *Ten dogs in the window.* New York: North-South Books.

Norman, D. A. (1997). Melding mind and machine. *Technology Review, 100,* 29–31.

Rosenblatt, L. (1978). *The reader, the text, the poem: The transactional theory of the literary work.* Carbondale and Edwardsville: Southern Illinois University Press.

Rosenblatt, L. (1995). *Literature as exploration* (5th ed.). New York: Modern Language Association of America.

Smith, F. (2004). *Understanding reading* (6th ed.). Mahwah, NJ: Lawrence Erlbaum Associates.

Spielvogel, J. (2006). *Discovering our past: Ancient civilizations.* New York: Glencoe/McGraw-Hill.

Tulving, E. (1985). How many memory systems are there? *American Psychologist, 40,* 385–398.

II

Teaching Students Strategies for Learning How to Predict

Merlyn is perhaps the most famous literary character to predict what is to come, as the young Arthur, the once and future king, learns. "Education is experience, and the essence of experience is self-reliance" (White, 1958, p. 39). Merlyn, in T. H. White's version of the Arthurian legend, has an advantage that Arthur does not share. He lives in reverse and explains to Arthur: "But I unfortunately was born at the wrong end of time, and I have to live backwards from in front, while surrounded by a lot of people living forwards from behind. Some people call it having second sight" (p. 28).

✤ COGNITIVE STRATEGIES AND INSTRUCTIONAL ROUTINES

Unlike Merlyn, readers don't have the advantage of living backward so they can see what's coming. However, as teachers, we can help individual readers explore the types of thinking in which predictions use important text cues. In doing so, student predictions are likely to become increasingly accurate. These predictions make use of important text cues, and thus are increasingly more accurate. From our own teaching and from observing hundreds of classroom teachers in actual classroom practice, we know of a number of cognitive strategies (presented in this section) that greatly facilitate student learning. We also know that when students experience difficulty in comprehending text, teachers can isolate specific prediction strategies and provide more precise instruction. As Fullan, Hill, and Crévola (2006) note, we don't need more prescriptive teaching, but rather more precision in our teaching. By focusing on predictions—both learning to predict and learning from predictions—precision teaching addresses the conceptual understandings—and sometimes the misunderstandings—of their students.

In Part II of the text, the cognitive or thinking strategies that promote effective predictions are explored along with examples of how a teacher might encourage these. The term *strategies* circulates widely in discussions among educators and in textbooks (Kragler,

Walker, & Martin, 2005); therefore, a distinction is drawn here that the authors have found useful. *Cognitive strategies are those that readers can consciously apply as they attempt to make sense of the texts they encounter.* As readers become increasingly proficient at selecting and applying a strategy, it becomes procedural and implicit; in other words, it becomes a skill (see Frey, Fisher, & Berkin, in press). Part III of this text will investigate the connection between the cognitive strategies teachers teach students to employ (e.g., predicting and summarizing) and the classroom structures or instructional routines (e.g., DR-TA and reciprocal teaching) teachers use to promote strategic thinking in student readers.

1 Attending to Text Features: Illustrations

Pictures attract readers' attention from the very first time a parent sits down to read a story out loud. In some texts, pictures serve as a cue for emergent readers who are still learning that letters and sounds have a correspondence and that those correspondences are a foundation for reading. In other stories, like one of the examples in this section, the pictures themselves tell the stories. When pictures or illustrations are present, readers who learn to pay attention to particular attributes of the text and the artwork can make predictions about what happens next as they move from page to page.

Years ago, in *The Read-Aloud Handbook*, Jim Trelease (1982) noted that picture books without words allow students to become familiar with the world of books, to imagine a world suggested by the pictures, and develop the idea of how stories progress. Although he is adamant about the idea that picture books serve a useful purpose for readers of all ages, Trelease states, "A good story is a good story, whether it has pictures or not" (2006, pp. 64–65).

LEARNING TO PREDICT

1. Call students' attention to the pictures, pointing out what attributes of the picture contribute to the story.

2. Ask students to fit picture cues with textual cues. Dechant (1991) suggests that early readers learn both word recognition and comprehension skills from attending to picture cues. When a young reader in the early stages of reading development encounters an unknown word, the teacher should help the reader identify important cues including explicit references to the pictures surrounding the text.

3. When reading a picture book, the teacher may employ a strategy we have adapted for predictions. It is simply called "How do you know?" (Richards & Anderson, 2003). During a read-aloud, the teacher stops at a place calling for a prediction. The students will respond, after which the teacher asks them, "Does the author say that?" When the students say, "No," the teacher follows up by asking them why they think their prediction will be accurate. Students are prompted to refer to all the cues. In using pictures, graphs, and charts, the teacher may ask students to refer to the graphic before responding by asking "Are there any pictures (or charts, etc.) that give you some clues?"

APPLICATIONS AND EXAMPLES

Elementary Classroom.   Barbara Dynes, a fourth-grade teacher, uses picture books to help students learn to predict and use homophones. At first, she introduces a few homophones like *ore* and *oar* and explores with the students that the words sound the same but have different meanings. She points out that a spell-checker in many word processing programs often will not catch a homophone that is used incorrectly. Then, she brings out the wordless picture book, *Eye Spy: A Mysterious Alphabet* (Bourke, 1991). In each picture, students must attend to cues that advance the mystery. As they work through the book, they become increasingly proficient at recognizing the cues that make prediction for the next letter possible.

IN HER OWN WORDS: Barbara Dynes, Etiwanda, California, Etiwanda Elementary School District

Lesson Overview: Learning to Predict with Homophones

Use the book, *Eye Spy: A Mysterious Alphabet* by Bourke (1991). This text will allow you to teach homophones but through a unique text feature—foreshadowing through illustrations that allow readers to predict what is to come.

1. Have students sit nearby so the pictures can be easily seen.
2. Tell students that they will use picture clues to solve puzzles about homophone riddles, and there is also a clue hidden in the last illustration on each right-hand page. That clue will lead to the next letter's puzzle. See Figures 1.1a and 1.1b.
3. Turn to the page that displays "A" and, while pointing at each illustration, say "ant, ant, ant, aunt." You may want to write these on a dry-erase board so students see the differences in spelling.
4. Ask students, "Who can guess what the next illustration will be?"
5. Hints can be given and will probably be necessary for the first few pages. The aunt's necklace includes a picture of two bowling pins, the subject of the page for the letter "B."
6. After the entire book is completed, review the book once again with the students calling out each illustration as the teacher points at each one.
7. The teacher asks for more examples of homophones and records them on the board.
8. At this point, the students select a pair of homophones and illustrate both meanings on a paper which has been folded in half. A class book can be assembled from the students' work.

Secondary Classroom.   United States History teacher Matt Duggan also uses illustrations and pictures to guide his students' predictions. During their examination of the Industrial Revolution, Mr. Duggan displayed a number of photos from this period in history. After considering a number of the pictures, Mr. Duggan asked students to talk with a partner about what they saw and what they could predict might be some of the problems the people would encounter. Walking around the room, Mr. Duggan heard a number of comments, including:

Figure 1.1 (**a**) Illustrations help readers predict in an alphabet book (**b**) Did you notice the bowling pins in the aunt's jewelry from the last frame?

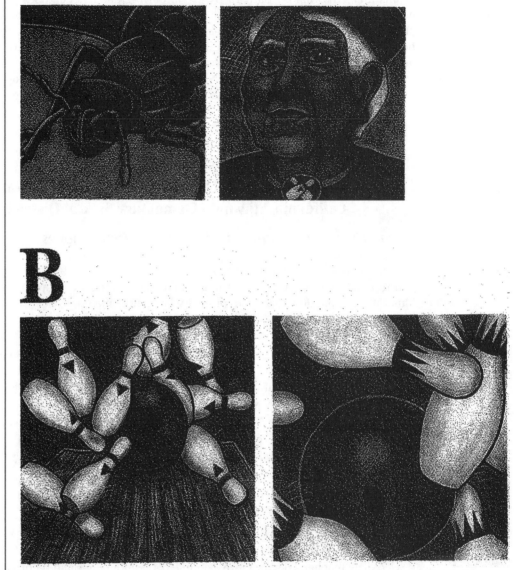

Source: Bourke, L. (1991). *Eye spy: A mysterious alphabet.* New York: Trumpet Club and Chronicle Books.

Tynesia: They look all dirty. They're gonna have problems with keeping clean and well.

Ricky: It's so crowded and dirty. Look at that one (points to a crowded factory). Those people don't have room.

James: The machines look so old. I've heard about this—they mangled people. Arms got ripped off and stuff. These machines were wicked.

Mr. Duggan was pleased with the discussions his students were having related to the illustrations and photographs. He knew that their predictions about the issues at hand would serve them well in building the necessary background knowledge to understand the texts they would be reading. He also noted that none of the partners talked about the age of the people in some of the photos. He asked the class a more pointed question: "Take a look again at the photos and illustrations around the room. You're seeing a lot of great stuff that will really help you comprehend the texts we're going to read and the unit overall. What I'm wondering about is the ages of people you're seeing in some of the visuals. Look at the kids. Why are there so many kids in the photos? What do you think that is about?"

After the students talked with their partners for a few minutes, Mr. Duggan interrupted them and introduced the idea of child labor. He talked for a few minutes about the ages of workers and how this has changed over time. He also showed a short film clip about child labor during the Industrial Revolution and asked his students to consider the spoken text of the film and the images. He knew that using visuals to build background knowledge by asking students to make predictions ensured their attention and learning.

2 Attending to Text Features: Tables, Diagrams, Graphs, and Charts

Texts that students use in learning content are often filled with tables, diagrams, graphs, and charts. Students can learn to use these features to help make sense of the materials they read and to make more informed predictions before and during reading. It is surprising that there is not a great deal of research on the linkage of text, comprehension, and diagrams. This appears to be true about many study aids and strategies that apply to content area reading and textbooks (Devine & Kania, 2003). One note: Throughout this book, we will distinguish between texts, which are any print material that students might encounter, and textbooks, which are materials written specifically for instructional purposes.

Diagrams and other visual aids provide cues to readers that can help them make more accurate predictions as they read. Figure 2.1 provides a list of common text features. A 1997 study (Moore & Scevak, 1997) found that students in fifth and seventh grade were less apt to attend to and connect the visual aids they encountered with the text they were reading than their ninth-grade counterparts. In part, visual aids provide a measure of redundancy, which can be a useful tool when we think about literacy (Burmark, 2002). A message that appears in more than one form or format is one to which a reader should pay increased attention. Visual aids may also help readers connect concepts represented in texts by visually presenting organizational patterns (Feathers, 1993). Finally, we can consider visual aids as texts in and of themselves independent of connected prose as it might be found in textbooks.

Figure 2.1   Common Text Features

Features That Organize the Text
Table of contents Index Glossary Page numbers
Features That Organize the Ideas
Synopses (beginning or end of reading) Titles Headings Subheadings Conclusion
Graphic Aids
Photographs Illustrations Diagrams Charts and tables Maps
Features That Elaborate or Emphasize
Captions Bold, italicized, or highlighted words Footnotes Margin notes
Features That Extend Understanding
Questions Summary Projects or assignments

LEARNING TO PREDICT

1. Students can benefit if their attention is specifically directed to the visual aids such as diagrams, pictures, graphs, tables, and charts because these are easily comprehensible forms of information that can help a student predict, and thus attend to, the concepts represented in the accompanying text.

2. Teachers can use a think-aloud protocol to model how to connect information gained from visual aids with the text. This action will reduce the uncertainty of predictions made during reading.

3. Students should take time to survey texts in advance of reading them, paying special attention to visual aids as well as annotations in text margins and font types (e.g., bold type font, italicized fonts, larger font than surrounding text, etc.). Teachers can encourage this practice by specifically directing students to survey the visual elements in their texts and by providing time for students to do so.

APPLICATIONS AND EXAMPLES

Elementary Classroom.   Punxsutawney Phil is the well-known groundhog who forecasts the arrival of spring. Maureen Marino's third-grade students decide to see how accurate Phil is. They read graphs and charts on CNN's weather page (Figure 2.2) to chart the highs and lows each day for the six-week period beginning on Groundhog Day, February 2. Students work in groups, with each group assigned to a different city and state. As their accumulated data increases, the students predict what the weather will be like and analyze topographical features for their effect on the weather.

The class discusses what it means to have "typical weather" for the particular time of year in their region. The students know that they are collecting data but need to investigate further what type of weather indicates an early spring or more winter weather. The students also create a chart with their data using Microsoft's Excel® spreadsheet. Once their data is entered, the students learn to create a bar graph, which Mrs. Marino's students use to test their predictions about the winter weather. (If doing this with older students, you may want to use the *Farmer's Almanac* to predict the weather, as well.) Mrs. Marino's students call their project P.H.I.L.: keep, "of course," Predictions Help Individual Learning (Figure 2.3a and 2.3b).

Figure 2.2   Weather Conditions

Figure 2.3a Zachary's Daily Chart of High and Low Temperatures

February

		Groundhog Day 02/02/06	1	2	3	4
				High 62°F Low 51°F ✓ type Show	High 59° Low 51°F ✓ type P/C	High 59°F Low 45°F ✓ type rain

	5	6	7	8	9	10	11
week 1	High 61°F Low 48°F ✓ type Sunn	High 57° Low 46°F ✓ type Sunn	High 60°F Low 49° ✓ type Sunn	High 60° Low 48° ✓ type Sun	High 70° Low 49° ✓ type Sunny	High 68°F Low 50°F ✓ type Sunn	High 62° Low 50° ✓ type P/C

	12	13	14	15	16	17	18
week 2	High 64° Low 49°F ✓ type Sunn	High 66° Low 48°F ✓ type Sunn	High 69°F Low 49°F ✓ type P/C	High 59° Low 49°F ✓ type P/C	High 54°F Low 41° ✓ type P/C	High 51°F Low 39°F ✓ type Show	High 52°F Low 39° ✓ type Show

	19	20	21	22	23	24	25
week 3	High 53° Low 39° ✓ type P/C	High 56° Low 40° ✓ type P/C	High 57° Low 42° ✓ type Sunn	High 60° Low 41°F ✓ type Sun	High 61° Low 46° ✓ type Sun	High 50° Low 47°F ✓ type Sun	High 65° Low 52° ✓ type P/C

	26	27	28	1	2	3	4
week 4	High 66° Low 53° ✓ type rain	High 60° Low 51°F ✓ type thun	High 63°F Low 50° ✓ type P/C	High 59° Low 46°F ✓ type P/C	High 55° Low 39° ✓ type Sun	High 53°F Low 43°F ✓ type Show	High 59° Low 51°F ✓ type P/C

March

	5	6	7	8	9	10	11
week 5	High 61°F Low 46° ✓ type rain	High 59° Low 49° ✓ type Show	High 56° Low 45° ✓ type Show	High 56° Low 49°F ✓ type P/C	High 54° Low 39°F ✓ type P/C	High 51° Low 37°F ✓ type Show	High 53°F Low 40° ✓ type Show

	12	13	14	15	16	17	18
week 6	High 55° Low 42°F ✓ type hail	High 55°F Low 39°F ✓ type P/C	High 57° Low 45° ✓ type thun	High 61° Low 47° ✓ type P/C			

Figure 2.3b   Zachary's Bar Graphs Created with a Spreadsheet Program

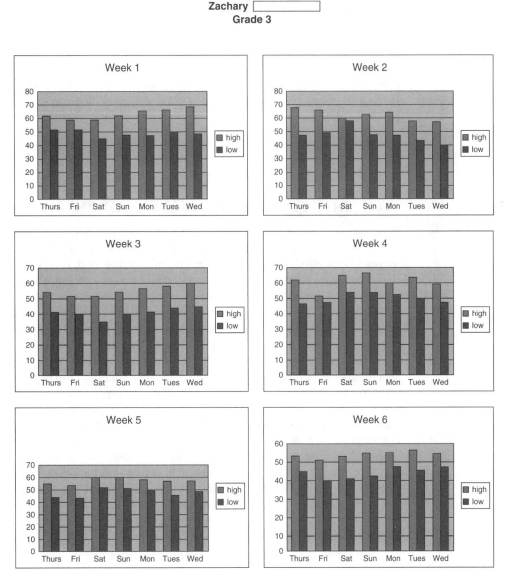

Secondary Classroom.   With older students in his science class, Jesse Herrera teaches his students to use text features to make predictions. While reading aloud from a science article, Mr. Herrera pauses to make a prediction based on an illustration and the caption underneath it. He models the use of text features and their usefulness in predicting, and thus comprehending, so that his students will incorporate this practice into their repertoires.

Looking at a photo of a scrawny tree, Mr. Herrera models predictions, "This tree doesn't look so good. I think the gardener needs to come and cut it down." He then reads the caption, which describes the tree as a "champion tree" and one that scientists would like to clone. He says, "Oh, a champion tree. Champion usually means that it's the winner. Given that word and the fact that scientists want to clone it, I predict this tree is important. I also predict that there will be problems, as I know that people are sometimes uncomfortable with cloning. I bet the author will tell us more about this as we read on."

Mr. Herrera knows that making predictions based on the visual information presented in texts helps students consolidate their thinking, motivates them to keep reading to check their predictions, and results in better comprehension. He also knows that modeling new or complex thinking, the use of predictions in this example, is an important way for students to incorporate this into their thinking habits.

3 Attending to Text Structures

Readers can learn a great deal from the content of a text. Students reading about the Constitutional Convention can learn about the important role George Washington played in moving the new nation forward, or discover that Thomas Jefferson, who wrote the early drafts of the Declaration of Independence, did not attend the Constitutional Convention. However, the structure of a text can also provide valuable information, too. From the text's structure, readers learn how ideas are related to each other and what might come next. Because text structure conveys information about how concepts are organized, it also provides a basis for predicting and learning from those predictions. Organization points readers in the direction of important attributes, making use of the schemata a reader already has and the schemata that develop as the reading continues.

First think of text structures as one of two types: texts that describe or texts affected by time (Dymock, 2005). Major rhetorical structures like description, sequence, cause and effect, and so on help readers determine just what type of information they are reading and how to make sense of these structures. Figure 3.1 contains a description of the major types of text structures. Chapter and section headings in most content area textbooks help students see how one idea is related to another, as well. We can think of story grammar as a means of paying attention to important elements of narratives, such as novels and short stories. Since predicting calls for attention to specific attributes of a text source, it is important for teachers to show students how texts are organized and how that organization can improve understanding.

LEARNING TO PREDICT

1. Survey the text. Model for students how to skim the text for organizational patterns and scan for key words. Project a page of text using a data or overhead projector, highlighting important indicators of text structure such as key words in bold or italics, or headings that are indented, in italics, in bold type, or in a different font.

2. Use notetaking tools (Fisher, Brozo, Frey, & Ivey, 2007) and demonstrate their use so that students detect and employ the structure of the text to organize the information they encounter. Concept maps use a series of bubbles or boxes to organize ideas in clusters (see section 3.10 for more on graphic organizers as they relate to predictions). Structured overviews are a type of concept map

Figure 3.1   Text Structure Types

Text Structure	Description	Signal Words
Description/List Structure	This structure resembles an outline. Each section opens with its main idea, then elaborates on it, sometimes dividing the elaboration into subsections. EXAMPLE: A book may tell all about whales or describe what the geography is like in a particular region.	For example, for instance, specifically, in particular, in addition
Cause and Effect Structure	In texts that follow this structure, the reader is told the result of an event or occurrence and the reasons it happened. EXAMPLE: Weather patterns could be described that explain why a big snowstorm occurred.	Consequently, therefore, as a result, thereby, leads to
Comparison/ Contrast Structure	Texts that follow this structure tell about the differences and similarities of two or more objects, places, events, or ideas by grouping their traits for comparison. EXAMPLE: A book about ancient Greece may explain how the Spartan women were different from the Athenian women.	However, unlike, like, by contrast, yet, in comparison, although, whereas, similar to, different from
Order/Sequence Structure	Texts that follow this structure tell the order in which steps in a process or series of events occur. EXAMPLE: A book about the American revolution might list the events leading to the war. In another book, steps involved in harvesting blue crabs might be told.	Next, first, last, second, another, then, additionally

Source: Using Text Structure, National Education Association, www.nea.org/reading/usingtextstructure.html. Used with permission.

Figure 3.2   Freytag's Pyramid

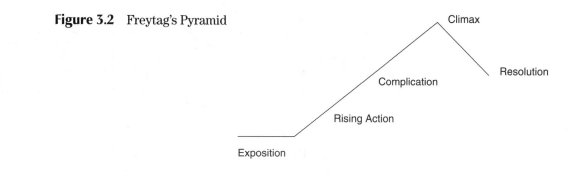

frequently presented as prereading. The graphics are best presented in written and oral form by the teacher prior to students being asked to read. In this way, students become familiar with the organization of ideas in the text and more readily connect the concepts as they read.

3. Make use of story grammar. Story grammar helps students by expanding elements of the story (conflict, characters, plot, and so on) for individual examination. A graphic which may help students to understand the plot of a story is based on Freytag's pyramid (Figure 3.2).

4. Students should be provided opportunities to reflect (Dymock, 2005) on the text structures they have encountered. Teachers can promote reflection through questions about what text structures were encountered, how a graphic organizer helps students to connect and visualize the organizational structures, and whether the structure was appropriate for the content.

APPLICATIONS AND EXAMPLES

Elementary Classroom.   During their small group reading instruction, Ms. Allen asked her students to focus on the structure of the text to help them predict what the author might tell them next. As they read *Lightning* (Kramer, 1992), the students in this fifth-grade class paused to talk with each other and their teacher about the description of lightening. They noted that the author used a lot of words to "tell us what he saw and heard and felt," as Javier noted. Amanda added that she thought he would do the same thing, add a lot of description, but also use "compare and contrast because next in the book we're learning about thunder. I think Mr. Kramer will compare thunder and lightening **and** give us lots of details about thunder. That's what I think."

Secondary Classroom.   Social studies call for understanding the relationships between concepts as they are presented in texts. Mr. Wolsey presented a structured overview of taxes the British Parliament levied on American colonists (Figure 3.3). Then the students used double-entry journals to help them organize their thoughts as they read the text and observed the relationships between the concepts. As students read the textbook, they were able to use the knowledge they obtained from the structured overview to help them navigate the text (Figures 3.4a and 3.4b).

Figure 3.3 Structured Overview: Pre-Revolution Taxes Imposed on American Colonists

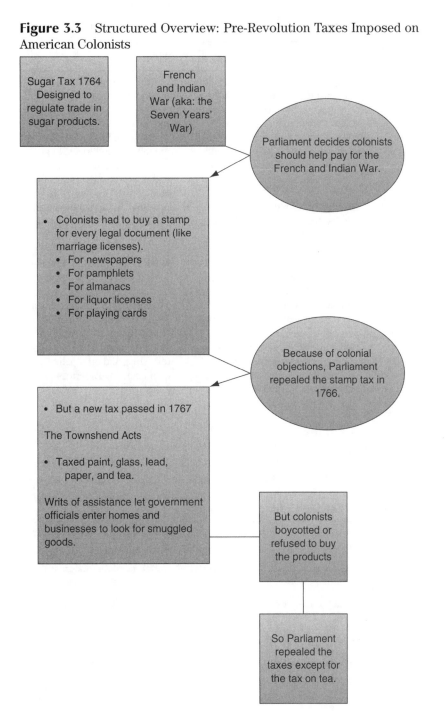

Figure 3.4a Source Text for Double-Entry Journal

Business Takes a New Direction

By the late 1800s, what we call "big business" came to dominate industry. Big business refers to an establishment that is run by entrepreneurs who finance, manufacture, and distribute goods. As time passed, some big businesses came to control entire industries.

Rise of Big Business

New technologies required the investment of large amounts of money, or capital. To get the needed capital, owners sold **stock,** or shares in their companies, to investors. Each stockholder became owner of a tiny part of a company. Large-scale companies, such as steel foundries, needed so much capital that they sold hundreds of thousand of shares. These businesses formed giant **corporations,** businesses that are owned by many investors who buy shares of stock. With large amounts of capital, corporations could expand into many areas.

Move Toward Monopolies

Powerful business leaders created monopolies and trusts, huge corporate structures that controlled entire industries or areas of the company in Germany, Alfred Krupp inherited a steelmaking business from his father. He bought up coal and iron mines as well as ore deposits—supply lines or raw materials that fed the steel business. Later, he and his son acquired plants that made tools, railroad cars, and weapons. In the United States, John D. Rockefeller built Standard Oil Company into an empire. By gaining control of oil wells, oil refineries, and oil pipelines, he dominated the American petroleum industry.

Figure 3.4b Double-Entry Notes

	Chapter 9: Life in the Industrial Age	
	In what ways did business change direction?	*Some businesses controlled entire industries (like steel production)*
	How did big business become so dominant?	*New technology required a lot of money, so stockholders contributed money and became part owners of the company. These eventually became huge corporations.*
	What are monopolies and how did they form?	*Monopolies control many aspects of an industry destroying competition. Germany: Krupp's steelmaking business bought coal and iron mines to feed his business. US: Rockefeller bought oil wells, refineries, & pipelines. Became Standard Oil.*

Source: Ellis, E. G. & Esler, A. (2007). *World history: The modern era.* Upper Saddle River, NJ: Pearson Prentice Hall.

4 Attending to Literary Devices

Literary devices include a wide variety of techniques employed by an author to add depth and create a sense of verisimilitude in a work of literature, often fiction. Because literary devices, such as flashbacks or metaphors, provide a framework for a work of literature or for a segment of a work, the readers who know a literary device is in use can also use that knowledge to engage with the text. A list of common literary devices can be found in Figure 4.1. This knowledge, in turn, provides a framework the reader may use to determine the important attributes of the text and make predictions that are increasingly accurate.

LEARNING TO PREDICT

1. Students need to know what the literary device is and how it is employed. This should not be a guessing game for students. Learners need assistance in determining what the relevant attributes are for a given problem (Gick & Holyoak, 1983; Holyoak & Thagard, 1995). If a teacher wants students to identify a relevant metaphor, then students' attention needs to be explicitly drawn to that metaphor. Sending students on a protracted search for a metaphor that the teacher already has in mind frequently ends in frustration for both the teacher and the students.

2. Once students recognize a particular literary device in a work of literature, they are then in a position to use that knowledge to make predictions about what might happen and how that contributes to other aspects of literary experience. In *The Outsiders* (Hinton, 1967), the main character wonders early in the story what it is like to be inside a burning ember as he lights a cigarette. Teachers can help students as novice readers to recognize this as foreshadowing events that occur later in the work, which add depth to the story and assist savvy readers to know something about that character, Ponyboy. Later in the novel, Ponyboy does end up inside a burning church saving some children from the flames. This event is pivotal as the plot develops.

3. Students can be encouraged to make a note of these literary devices as they are encountered and when the teacher or a peer points them out by using a literature response journal. In this way, students become more conversant with the vocabulary of literary devices and the concepts those terms represent.

APPLICATIONS AND EXAMPLES

Secondary Classroom.   Jason Lefevre wants his high school students to use literary devices to enrich their experience with the novella, *A River Runs Through It* (Maclean, 1976). He writes about teaching students of "spots of time," a term given to any moment in one's life that has occurred in the past and has not been fully understood as to the influential qualities the moment had on the person's life. In this example, Mr. Lefevre uses questions to point out elements of the plot that may foreshadow future events in the story.

Figure 4.1 Literary Terms That Lead to Better Predictions

Metaphors.   Because an author employs metaphors to draw attention to both the meaning conveyed and to attributes of the larger story, metaphors, as literary devices, may also help direct students' attention to important elements of a poem, short story, or novel. Sandburg's famous poem mourning the loss of Abraham Lincoln is an extended metaphor. When the poet writes in "O Captain, My Captain":

> O Captain! my Captain! our fearful trip is done, The ship has weathered every rack, the prize we sought is won,

The reader's attention is focused on a difficult journey and the leader who guided the passengers safely home. In this poem, the vehicle of the metaphor is a ship in a storm-tossed sea and the tenor of the poem is the grief felt at the loss of a beloved leader.

Similes.   Like metaphors, similes compare two unlike objects. And like metaphors, knowledge of how similes are employed in a written work can assist the reader by directing attention. Similes differ from metaphors in that the comparison is stated directly. In Sandburg's poem, prior knowledge must be employed to infer that the poem is about Lincoln. In Robert Burns' famous line, "O My luve's like a red, red rose," there is no question what is being compared.

Foreshadowing.   Literary devices that are presented in literature which lay the groundwork for later events are known as foreshadowing. In Shakespeare's *Macbeth*, the witches in Act I, Scene I chant:

> "Fair is foul, and foul is fair, Hover through the fog and filthy air." The reader learns in Scene III that the witches are very talented at causing confusion. Witch 2 tells Macbeth's companion, Banquo, that he is, "Lesser than Macbeth, and greater." Banquo's role in the tragedy of Macbeth is foreshadowed and the savvy reader knows to pay attention to this character.

Flashbacks.   This literary device presents events that occurred chronologically before the opening scene or main timeline of the narration. Flashbacks provide important information that is critical to understanding the events of the story to come and the nature of the characters that populate the story. Able readers of literature pay attention any time the timeline skips backward because it will provide significant details that can inform predictions about the motivation of characters and the subsequent events of the story. Methods of taking the reader along during the flashback include "recollections of characters, narration by the characters, dream sequences, and reveries" (Holman & Harmon, 1992, p. 197).

Norman Maclean uses the fishing streams of his childhood to contemplate the emotions he feels about his deceased brother. This is an example of a "spot of time" in Norman Maclean's life. Maclean chooses to write about his brother's death more than 30 years after the murder happens, after life's experiences have shaped his thoughts about his brother's life and death.

Mr. Lefevre asks his students to predict what they think the novella *A River Runs Through It* is about based on the information he has given them and the novella's title. Mr. Lefevre's students are comfortable working in pairs and he asks them to read and clarify what they think they are reading. When Norman's brother gambles incessantly, do they think this is a foreshadowing of what is going to happen? Mr. Lefevre's students seem to do a good job of predicting the more obvious points of a piece, but they have trouble with the thematic objectives of the author. He guides his students' understanding of the role of fishing as a family to the novella. As he clarifies some of the more obscure points of the novella, other areas of the story will become easier for the students to understand.

 ### *IN HIS OWN WORDS:* Jason Lefevre, The Salisbury School, Salisbury, Connecticut

Norman MacLean uses the fishing streams of his childhood to contemplate the emotions he feels about his deceased brother. This is an example of a "spot of time" in Norman MacLean's life. MacLean chooses to write about his brother's death more than 30 years after the murder happens, after life's experiences have shaped his thoughts about his brother's life and death.

I will ask my students to predict what they think the novella *A River Runs Through It* is about based on the information I have given them and the title of the novella. I have already put my students in pairs and asked them to read and clarify what they think they are reading. When Norman's brother gambles incessantly, do they think this is a foreshadowing of what is going to happen? My students seem to do a good job of predicting the more obvious points of a piece, but they have trouble with the thematic objectives of the author. I will need to help my students understand the role of fishing as a family to the novella. As I clarify some of the more obscure points of the novella, other areas of the story will become easier for my students to understand.

Elementary Classroom.   Literary devices are not the sole realm of secondary school English teachers. Authors use literary devices all of the time, across texts that people of all ages read. During her small group reading instruction, Ms. Allen asked her fifth-grade students to notice the author's use of color as a symbol in the book *Rose Blanche* (Innocenti, 1985). Noticing the colors the author used in the text allowed students to develop their sense of symbolism and to better understand the subtle transitions the author was making as the story progressed. As Tino noted while reading this text, "Oh, the sky changed to grey here. That's not a good sign. I think that some things are gonna happen that are even worse than the trucks in the streets and the soldiers being strict."

5 Accessing and Activating Background Knowledge

When teachers discuss what students already know prior to learning something new, they generally use one of two terms: *background knowledge* and *prior knowledge.* Most of the time, the two terms are employed interchangeably (Strangman & Hall, 2004). In this book, we will differentiate between background knowledge and prior knowledge as follows: Background knowledge is that which the learner has acquired as a result of lived experiences. Students in the Midwest may have very limited background knowledge about the beach, for example. Likewise, a student who grew up in a city may not have the schema necessary to understand a text passage about a farm.

Prior knowledge, in contrast, is that which a student learns as a result of being in school. What a student learned from a book last week or a lab experiment last year is prior knowledge. This distinction becomes important when teachers plan instruction for their students.

Before moving on, one more point should be made. A good prediction is not necessarily one that turns out to be correct. An operational definition is as follows: A good prediction is one that relies on relevant attributes and knowledge the student already has to increasingly reduce uncertainty. A prediction that ultimately turns out to be incorrect may still be a good prediction if the reader is able to learn from the prediction while proceeding through the text.

Many textbooks used in teacher preparation programs suggest that teachers take steps before students read to prepare them for challenging materials (e.g., Alvermann & Phelps, 2005; Betts, 1946; Ryder & Graves, 2003; Tompkins, 2003; Vacca & Vacca, 2005). This may be known as preparation for reading, prereading, or simply "before" reading. The idea that what students already know is the foundation for what they are to learn is not new. Some implications for teachers are:

1. Students may have knowledge that is relevant but remains untapped in a given lesson.
2. Students may not make adjustments accounting for new information if the knowledge they already have interferes.
3. Students may experience interference when teaching practices don't match their lived experiences (Bransford, Brown, & Cocking, 2000).

Smith and Wilhelm's (2002) interesting study of literacy and boys' lives suggests that teachers who recognize the outside interests of their students also foster a sense of competence that reaches beyond merely building relationships. Teachers can plan lessons that take their students' background knowledge into account. Planning appropriate activities and experiences before students read can help improve the reading experience, and thus comprehension, of the text.

LEARNING TO PREDICT

1. The cultural knowledge that students bring to school with them affects the new knowledge they are able to construct. Teachers should consider factors

that extend beyond class, race, or ethnicity and take care to avoid stereotypes about their students, of course. Teachers who know what their students know do far more than administer an interest survey or background inventory at the beginning of the year. In order to know their students, teachers who assist their students to construct new knowledge take the time to talk regularly with their students as individuals—when they enter the classroom each day, as they move about the room when students are working, and at lunch.

2. All reading, even on the most literal of levels, requires the reader to activate appropriate schema (Anderson, 2004). Students without the right schema to draw upon or who activate the wrong schema will not comprehend the text. Consider this sentence:

> A loop knot is a closed bight that is tied either in the end or in the central part of the rope. (Ashley, 1944, p. 185)

To make sense of this sentence, one has to know what a *bight* is and how it relates to tying knots. Without that background knowledge, this passage won't make sense. A reader could also confuse *bight* for *bite* because the pronunciations are the same. Such confusion would eliminate the chance that much comprehension would take place. For teachers, this means instructing students in monitoring their comprehension of concepts they encounter that don't make sense. Teachers who know their students and the content of the reading material will take steps to teach students in advance of the students reading those concepts that might be confusing.

3. When students' attention is directed in ways that improve comprehension, they are free to concentrate on the cognitive tasks of making predictions and looking for connections within the text. Students who struggle with matching their background knowledge to the concepts in the text exhaust their cognitive resources before they can work on constructing meaning at other levels.

APPLICATIONS AND EXAMPLES

Secondary Classroom. Hilary Biggers' students are preparing to read a play. Although she knows that some concepts in the play will be outside the realm of experience for her students, she wanted them to engage with the play's ideas.

 ## *IN HER OWN WORDS:* Nyree Clark, Colton Joint Unified School District

Background Knowledge in a Kindergarten Class

A topic in the kindergarten science standards is earth science. The students must know the difference between different landforms. We are learning about mountains. The first thing I did was have a discussion about mountains. I asked the students a series of questions such as, "Do you know what a mountain is? What does it look like? What can you do there? What kinds of animals live there?" While the students talked I wrote their responses on a large chart paper. I also asked the students if any of them have been to the mountains and what did they do when they were there. We talked about living in the mountains and visiting. The students also discussed what the mountains were like in the summer and what the mountains were like in the winter. After we discussed mountains I took them outside to actually look at the mountains. We took paper and sat on the ground and colored a picture of how the mountains looked outside. When the students finished their picture they wrote a story about it. When we came back inside I read them a story about mountains, building background knowledge, and we connected our responses from the chart paper to the story we were reading.

The reading selection is a screenplay of a *Twilight Zone* episode created by Rod Sterling entitled "Back There." The screenplay describes a young man's unintended travel back in time from April 14, 1965, to April 14, 1865, the day of President Lincoln's assassination. He attempts, yet fails, to stop the murder and is returned to 1965 where he declares that history cannot be changed. However, a character from his life prior to the time travel the readers meet in Act I, Scene I, has become a millionaire because of the main character's actions in 1865. The play has two acts and is taught in two separate lessons.

Before the students are introduced to the selection, their background knowledge is built by watching the "Eye of the Beholder" episode of *The Twilight Zone*. This prepares them for Rod Sterling's science fiction writing style and stimulates them to look for his subtle criticisms of society in "Back There." During their reading of the screenplay, several students in Ms. Biggers' class comment on the structure of science fiction in general and Mr. Sterling's use in particular. These students, the ones with extensive background knowledge of science fiction, are able to understand the text because they use their background knowledge to make predictions about the structure of the text and what is likely to happen in this genre. They also build the knowledge base of their peers as they explain their predictions and how they use their knowledge of time travel, for example, to understand the text.

Elementary Classroom.   Knowing that her students all had different experiences with city and country life, Ms. Schwartz selected the tale *City Mouse and Country Mouse* (Wallner, 1987) to read with her students. Since Ms. Schwartz knew that her students would have a different experience with mice, country life, and city life, she felt that this would be a great opportunity for her kindergarten students to share what they knew with one another and to build their collective knowledge base.

6   Accessing and Activating Prior Knowledge

In cognitive student strategy 5, we discussed the importance of background knowledge and some ways that teachers can make use of what students already know. Prior knowledge, learning that students gain as a result of their school experiences, is equally important. We can think about the role of prior knowledge in two ways: activating what is already known and building new knowledge, which serves as prior knowledge when students read. Teachers who collaborate with each other and who know something of what others teach increase the probability that their students will be able to activate that knowledge from other content areas or earlier grade levels in service of reading. As with background knowledge, what a teacher does before the students read a given text is critical. Many of the classroom structures discussed in the next section are designed, among other things, to activate both background and prior knowledge.

LEARNING TO PREDICT

1. Pay attention to vocabulary that is derived from the selection students are about to read. There are many activities that promote vocabulary knowledge, though these are beyond the scope of this book. Students who have learned something about the vocabulary they will encounter will read more fluently and with greater comprehension because they will not have to spend cognitive resources dealing with unfamiliar vocabulary. It helps to think of vocabulary as words that represent concepts from the content and are represented in the reading rather than as separate vocabulary-building activities that have no relation to the reading. In addition to classroom structures designed to introduce vocabulary or activate the prior knowledge the reader already has about the concept, teachers can facilitate word learning by using the words in speech with students (embedding the sentences with strategically placed synonyms), seeing the words written on chalkboards (we know—there are more and more white boards, these days), having students try out the words in small group activities, and so on.

2. When teaching content like social studies or science, teachers can facilitate building prior knowledge before students read by thinking about the activities already planned. For example, in science, a teacher may have planned a lab experience, a demonstration, and reading a course text. It may be beneficial for students to watch the demonstration or even participate in the lab before reading the material; the authentic experiences of the lab and demonstration build knowledge that will make reading a more meaningful experience for students. Reading about things that are somewhat familiar is reading that makes sense.

3. As with background knowledge, prior knowledge can help direct students' attention to important attributes of the content in the reading selection which enhances good predictions.

APPLICATIONS AND EXAMPLES

Secondary Classroom.   When Chad Semling's sixth-grade social studies students learn about economics, he introduces the important vocabulary from the text to them in advance with a strategy called "Meet and Greet." Note that some words will be familiar (such as *want*) while other terms will be fairly new (*recession*).

⚬⚬ *IN HIS OWN WORDS:* **Chad Semling, Menomonie Middle School, Menomonie, Wisconsin**

A Strategy to Pre-Assess Students' Vocabulary Knowledge

Economics Vocabulary: bond, barter, capital, consumer, depression, demand, dividend, economic interdependence, entrepreneur, equilibrium point, Federal Reserve Banks, gross domestic product, law of demand/supply, need, producer, recession, service, single proprietorship, and want

Words I Know	Words I Have Seen or Heard but Do Not Use	Words I Have Never Seen nor Heard.

Meet and Greet (Chapman & King, 2003) is such a simple yet seemingly effective way to pre-assess what students already know. The strategy presents a very clear picture of what vocabulary students do know and which words still need to be developed. Each student is presented with a list of words and then fills in a chart like the following one. Both teacher and student learn what words the student should attend to the most in developing their vocabulary and associated concepts.

Secondary Classroom: Analogy Boxes.   Analogy boxes (Rule & Furletti, 2004) are a concept learning tool teachers might use to improve how students compare what they learn with what they need to learn. Analogy boxes are included in this section about prior knowledge because students learn to find and compare common attributes of an analog and target. Students also learn content that improves the prior knowledge they can bring to bear in approaching reading tasks. To create analogy boxes, teachers make a set of cards from a current unit of study that represents an analog including a form and a function. Then, the teacher creates a card that corresponds to the target concept. The cards are placed in a box, hence "analogy boxes."

When students are given the boxes, they must select a target card and sort through the analog cards to find an analogous relationship. Once this is done, students map the analogy showing the relations of the analogy; in the example, this is done by underlining. In the final step, students create a chart showing the target, the analogy, and the similarities and the differences. Students might also be asked to provide an alternate analog other than the one provided on the analog cards (Figure 6.1).

Elementary Classroom.   During their unit on "people who make a difference," second-grade teacher Heather Mills wanted her students to read a number of biographies

Figure 6.1 Analogy Boxes for Earthquake Fault Types

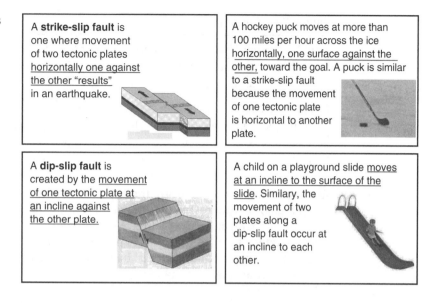

about famous Americans. She planned to extend this unit of study to people who have made a difference across the world and across time. However, based on her students' background knowledge, she decided to focus on people that her students knew personally. She started the unit with a class discussion about the idea, "people who make a difference." Ms. Mills asked, "Who is it that has made a difference in your lives and what did those people do?" The class discussion was lively and Ms. Mills recorded the many responses on a language chart. The language chart would serve as a record of the class knowledge that each student could refer back to during his or her personal investigation. Over several discussions, the class agreed upon characteristics of people who made a difference, including: cares, didn't get paid to do it, was in the right place, and so on.

As they selected the American who made a difference to profile, students used their prior knowledge and new information about characteristics to make predictions about the people they were studying. During their small group discussions about the Americans they studied, they extended their prior knowledge by adding to the characteristics with examples.

Eventually, when they studied people around the world who had made a positive impact, the students had developed significant prior knowledge such that they predicted what the biographies would contain and where to find the information they were looking for.

7 Noting Word-Level Cues

Mature readers rely on a variety of strategies to read words (Ehri, 1995; Ehri & McCormick, 2004). Experienced readers recognize most words on sight, having approached them through various other channels such as decoding or word roots and affixes. Dechant (1991) characterizes this process of recognizing words on sight as instant recognition. Less experienced readers and experienced readers who encounter a

Figure 7.1   Definitions

> **Syntactic cue:** Evidence from knowledge of the rules and patterns of language that aids in the identification of an unknown word from the way it is used in a grammatical construction (p. 249).
>
> **Semantic cue:** Evidence from the general sense or meaning of a written or spoken communication that aids in the identification of an unknown word (p. 229).

Source: From *The Literacy Dictionary*, Harris & Hodges, 1995.

new word may decode a word; that is, readers associate sounds with letters and letter clusters and reproduce the pronunciation for a word. Readers may also employ analogies to compare unknown words with known words based on spelling patterns. A fourth strategy for reading words is prediction based on initial letters in the words, the words that occur before and after the target word in the text, and perhaps based on the pictures that accompany the text (refer back to cognitive student strategy 1 for more about picture cues).

Analogies, as we pointed out in Part I, have predictive uses. A reader who knows several words by sight including *talk, walk,* and *chalk* can apply the knowledge, by analogy, to a new word, even replicating the silent "l" in *balk.* Readers who know many words by sight are able to learn more words through analogy, adding flesh to the argument that we learn to read by reading.

Syntax and semantic information also are useful as predictive tools for readers encountering a new word. One study found that fifth-grade students who were taught context analysis skills could generalize those skills to other texts when the texts were similar in nature, but that students didn't necessarily employ the use of context cues in more generalized reading situations (Baumann, Edwards, Boland, Olejnik, & Kame'enui, 2003). The researchers further taught students about five types of context cues (see Figure 7.1) which rely on semantic cues; the authors of this text added one which relies on syntactic cues.

LEARNING TO PREDICT

Baumann et al. (2003) taught the fifth-grade students in their study a two-pronged approach to attack a new word for meaning. Our Three-step adaptation asks students to:

1. Read the words and sentences around the unknown word for clues to meaning.
2. Look at the word parts for root words and affixes that are familiar.
3. Return to the words and sentences around the target or unknown word again to see if the readers came up with a word meaning that fits the context (Figure 7.2).

APPLICATIONS AND EXAMPLES

Elementary Classroom.   Teacher Rita Hanson wants her first-grade students to use context cues and the initial letter to make sense of a poem.

Figure 7.2   Using Context Clues

1. Definition of context clues: the author gives you a definition for a word right in the sentence.
2. Synonym context clues: The author uses another word that means about the same as the word you are trying to understand.
3. Antonym context clues: The author uses another word that means the opposite or nearly the opposite of the word you are trying to understand.
4. Example context clues: The author gives you several words or ideas that are examples of the word you are trying to understand.
5. General context clues: The author gives you some general clues to the meaning of a word, most often spread over several sentences.
6. To this, the authors of this book add word order clues: The order of the words can tell you if a word is a noun, an adjective (description), and so on.

Source: Adapted from Baumann, J. F., Edwards, E. C., Boland, E. M., Olejnik, S, & Kame'enui, E. J., (2003), p. 465.

IN HER OWN WORDS: Rita Hanson, Hanson School District, Alexandria, South Dakota

Title of Lesson: Using the beginning letter

Subject: Reading/First-grade large group

Literacy Objective: The children will use the beginning letter of a word in their reading to help them determine an unknown word. The lesson will also focus on using context clues to make sure words look right and make sense as students are reading.

Materials and resources: A large copy of the poem "Falling Up" written on chart paper big enough for all the students to see.

Anticipatory Set: Boys and girls, today I need your help reading the poem on the board. Someone has covered up some of the words in the poem. I was wondering if you could help me try to figure out those words that are covered up. Remember how when we read we have to make sure the words we are reading make sense and look right. Word detectives, are you ready to get to work?

Instructional Input: We will read the poem together using context clues to determine the covered word. I will use large sticky notes to hide certain words in the passage. The children will make attempts at the hidden words by using context clues. I will read the passage to them saying "blank" to signify the unknown words. The children will guess possible words that would make sense in the paragraph. The class will reread the sentence after each guess to make sure it makes sense and the word is about the right size. After four to five words have been attempted I will uncover the first letter of the word. I write all the attempted words on the board for them. We will discuss as a class what words can be eliminated because they do not have the correct beginning letter. The students will be given another opportunity to generate additional word possibilities (three to four) for the hidden word. I will uncover the covered word at this time to show the children the correct word.

Modeling: I will read the first sentence with the covered word. I will model for them through a think-aloud how a good reader thinks about what makes sense and looks right as they are reading.

Secondary Classroom.   Chad Semling approaches vocabulary in a unit on economics using a strategy called Crisscross Challenge (Chapman & King, 2003, p. 102). In economics, students encounter terms that have new meanings for words they already recognize (words like *bond, demand,* and *depression*) and new words students have never seen before (words like *dividend, entrepreneur,* and *gross domestic product*). In this example, Mr. Semling has students employ the glossary in the social studies textbook his seventh graders use along with context cues from the sentence where the target word is located in the text itself.

IN HIS OWN WORDS: Chad Semling, Menomonie Middle School, Menomonie, Wisconsin

This strategy involves a pair of students working together to accomplish a common goal, finding the term(s) both in the chapter and the glossary. Once the students find the locations, they read aloud the information they found. I feel this strategy serves a number of different purposes. First, it reinforces the idea of using a textbook's glossary. Second, the students see first hand not only a term's definition but also its contextual use. Literacy objectives met here would be: reading to perform a task and expressing ideas that build off the ideas of others. This may take modeling on my end, but students end up discussing the differences/similarities between what is in the glossary and what is in the chapter.

Chapman and King suggest that the Crisscross Challenge pits student teams against each other. The teacher posts a word, which the partners then locate in the text and glossary. When both are pointing to the location of the word in their respective sources, they shout "Crisscross" together. The partners read their information to the class and points may be accumulated for each team. All students can then use the glossary definition and context of the sentence or paragraph to explain the meaning of the word to each other.

Making Inferences

Inferences are close cognitive cousins of predictions. In each, thinkers are required to identify relevant attributes of one or more concepts and connect those attributes with other concepts. Teachers reading this book will probably recognize the situation of asking students to respond to questions only to find that they have copied passages from the text, word-for-word. Students who copy responses in this manner are often identifying key words from the question and matching them to a section of the text that contains those words. Often, what the teacher wants is for students to infer a response rather than literally recognize what had already been read. Indeed, students may expect that copying word-for-word is how one is supposed to respond to such questions. Students must learn not just what an inference is or that it is essential to comprehension; students must also "understand that they are making an inference about something" (Liben & Liben, 2005, p. 403) and when doing so is appropriate.

In making an inference, readers learn to connect their own existing knowledge with what they read (also referred to as scriptally implicit inferences) or to connect parts of the text with other parts of the text (also referred to as textually implicit). Each type of inference must be modeled and taught intentionally (McGee & Johnson, 2003) if students are to avoid the trap of no words "Identifying" means something else stick with "calling" words accurately but not really comprehending the text. To further complicate the skill of making inferences, readers must also be able to do so at the word, sentence, and event levels (the focal level, borrowing from Smith, 2004) or for the text as a whole (the global level). We can look at inferences by comparing them with their purposes (Table 8.1).

An elaborative inference requires the reader to predict a possible outcome for events, add detail by relating personal experiences to those related in the text, and so on. As such, these inferences add depth to a reader's understanding of the text through elaboration. Cohesive inferences require readers to make use of connective features of sentences and larger text structures, such as paragraphs. In the sentence, "I lost my book, but Jan found it under the sofa," the reader must infer that "it" is the book, which was found under the sofa. This is a focal prediction of the cohesive type.

Often students reading a textbook must hold in mind concepts from earlier in the text and connect those with concepts recently encountered. This is done in working memory (Cain, Oakhill, & Bryant, 2004) where integration enabling inferences takes place. You may wish to review the role of working memory presented earlier in this book. Clearly, readers who have learned to attend to appropriate attributes of a reading selection and who also have learned to deploy their attention in working memory appropriately are more apt to make inferences that span large sections of text, from one

Table 8.1   Types of Inferences

Elaborative Inference	Not necessary for comprehension	Scriptally implicit (relies on background knowledge)
Cohesive Inference	Necessary for comprehension	Textually implicit (relies primarily on cues at the word, sentence, or whole text level)
Knowledge-Based Inference	Necessary for comprehension	Scriptally implicit
Evaluative Inferences	Necessary for comprehension	Scriptally implicit (relies on background knowledge and calls for the reader to relate an emotional connection to the text.

Adapted from Bowyer-Crane & Snowling, 2005.

paragraph to another, from one chapter to another, and so on. These are also types of cohesive inferences.

Knowledge-based inferences require readers to draw on background knowledge in order to understand what they are reading. Consider this passage: "When I opened the book, I found that the title page was torn. Jan ran to get the tape." In this sentence, background knowledge is required which would suggest to the reader that tape is used to repair torn pages, and Jan will locate this resource to help me effect the repair. None of this is stated in the passage. It must be inferred, and from this example teachers will be able to infer that students who ask why the author doesn't just come right out and say what they mean would end up writing a huge tome, explicating every little detail.

In a more complicated example of the knowledge-based inference, consider the opening lines of Hemingway's story, "A Day's Wait" (1987, p. 332).

> He came into the room to shut the windows while we were still in bed
> and I saw he looked ill. He was shivering, his face was white, and he
> walked slowly as though it ached to move.

In the very first lines, we must infer that there are two people ("we") still in bed and a third walks into the room. This person could be a child (who else would just walk into the room?) or a butler (who else would be shutting windows?). We use background knowledge to make these inferences. But, we're not sure which of the two inferences is correct. What we must do is continue to read to see if we can obtain additional information that will help us determine who is shutting the windows first thing in the morning (another inference—is it really morning?). Let's read on.

> "What's the matter, Schatz?"
>
> "I've got a headache."
>
> "You better go back to bed."
>
> "No. I'm all right."
>
> "You go to bed. I'll see you when I'm dressed."
>
> But when I came downstairs he was dressed, sitting by the fire, looking
> a very sick and miserable boy of nine years. When I put my hand on his
> forehead, I knew he had a fever." (p. 332)

If you're thinking what we're thinking, then you know that Schatz is the boy's name, that the narrator of the story is probably the boy's father [we will have to keep reading to verify this prediction and inference], and you know that the butler is not the closer of morning windows (if it really is morning—we have to keep reading). All of these inferences were made with background knowledge about family relationships, story structures (the narrator refers to himself as "I," but we haven't yet verified the gender of the narrator, have we?), and that butlers are not typically nine years old. More important, we can use these inferences to make additional predictions about what happens in the next paragraph, the next page, and the rest of the story. When we connect the fact that Schatz refers to the narrator as "Papa" on page 333, we have made a cohesive inference connecting one part of the text on page 332 with another on page 333. The narrator is the father of the sick boy.

In "A Day's Wait," Hemingway's Schatz character mistakes degrees centigrade for degrees Fahrenheit and believes that he is going to die because his temperature is so high. Hemingway never tells us directly that Schatz is a brave boy who faces what he feels is impending death with a large measure of dignity, but readers of this story can relate their own emotional experiences of having a sick child or of being very sick to that of Schatz. In this case, the reader has made an evaluative inference that can inform a judgment; specifically, about the theme of the story.

LEARNING TO PREDICT

1. Teachers should model the process of connecting background knowledge and text segments with new information as reading progresses. This can be done by "thinking aloud," a process of explaining what the teacher is thinking aloud just as we have done in print in the previous passage.

2. Students can be taught there are different types of inferences and that inferences can help a reader predict what is going on in a text, thereby increasing attention to the relevant details of the text.

3. Students who have many opportunities to make inferences and to share those with classmates are increasingly likely to make what Allbritton terms predictive inferences (2004). This may include the use of small group discussions (e.g., Daniels, 1994, 2002), threaded discussions (Grisham & Wolsey, 2006; Wolsey, 2004), or literature response journals.

4. Teachers can provide or direct students to supporting information that builds schema (see Part IV) students may rely upon in making appropriate inferences.

APPLICATIONS AND EXAMPLES

Secondary Classroom.   Students in Dryer Thackston's high school English class read "Hair" by Malcolm X (1997), an essay in which the narrator describes the process some African Americans used to straighten their hair in the mid-twentieth century. Because the process involves substances that are unfamiliar to twenty-first century students and the essay deals with issues affecting African Americans before the civil rights era began in earnest, many inferences on the part of students are required. In the essay, Shorty is the friend who first conked Malcolm X's hair.

IN HIS OWN WORDS: Dryer Thackston, Watkins Mill High School, Gaithersburg, Maryland

A Conk Is More Than Just a Hair Style

These questions require students to connect text segments in order to make an inference (Cohesive, textually implicit):

The answers to the following questions are inferred by connecting information from different places in the text. You will have to answer them by making inferences.

1. How substantial is the amount of money that Malcolm X saves by having Shorty conk his hair? (Don't focus on the dollar amount—look for something in the story to compare with the barber's price for a conk.)

2. Why does Malcolm X curse at Shorty while his hair is being rinsed?

3. According to Malcolm X, what are the moral implications of conking one's hair?

These questions require students to connect information from the essay with their own background knowledge (knowledge-based and evaluative inferences, scriptally implicit):

You will have to use clues from the text as well as your own knowledge to answer these questions.

1. What purposes do the Vaseline, rubber apron, and gloves serve since they are not ingredients?

2. Why would African Americans at the time want to look "white"?

3. Why would Malcolm X call such African Americans "brainwashed"?

Elementary Classroom.   Reading between the lines, or making inferences, isn't easy for most students, yet it's a standard in most states. Understanding that inferring is important for students and is one of the ways that they make predictions, Leah Katz modeled inferring with her third-grade students. She used a number of comics from the newspaper to focus her students' attention on that which was left unsaid by the author/artist. After modeling the inferences she made on one panel of a comic strip, she asked students to talk with their partners about the next panel.

On one particular day, Ms. Katz's students were talking about the comic strip *Peanuts.* Dumas said to his partner, "I think that Charlie Brown will get in trouble. See the cloud coming and the darker lines? He didn't tell us that, but I think it will happen. I can make a prediction because of that. Because of the stuff that the author almost tells you."

9 Asking and Generating Questions

"To be, or not to be?" Hamlet's famous question (Act III, Scene I) also leads the reader to predict aspects of Hamlet's character. Hamlet is a confused, but thoughtful, prince. We might infer that, to him, questions were at least as important as answers. Questions and their answers, as we observe them in classrooms, characterize the discourse found there. Often, teachers ask questions and students respond. Thoughtful questions from teachers can provoke learning in ways no other instructional tool can. However, questions generated by students can be equally powerful, if not more so. We believe the ability to frame a thoughtful question, especially when the answer is not immediately known, is a skill teachers should encourage in their students. Of course, most readers of this book will be familiar with the questions that appear at the end of the section or chapter. These, too, can take a useful place in classroom discourse. In this section, we will treat statements that require a response as questions even if they aren't punctuated with a question mark at the end (Turner, 1983).

An interesting study (Daines, 1986) showed how 38 teachers in grades from 2 through 12 employed questions in their classrooms. The questions classified in this study were of four types: literal, interpretive, application, and affective. Interpretive questions included those that required students to make inferences, compare or contrast, determine cause and effect relationships, make predictions based on trends, and so on. Of the 5,289 questions teachers asked during this study, 93% were at the literal level. Less than 7% were interpretive questions. Teachers asked about 78 questions per hour, with second-grade teachers asking the most questions and tenth-grade teachers asking the fewest questions. On average, teachers only waited two seconds from the time the question was asked until a student responded; this time did not increase when higher-order questions were asked. Do you want to know how long the average student's response was? It was only three seconds, with a range that extended to five seconds in tenth grade.

Even though this study is more than 20 years old, the results can inform our teaching in the twenty-first century. First, we might expect that higher-order questions are asked when the questions are planned in advance, allowing for flexibility as a discussion evolves. Second, we can provide opportunities for students to think through their responses by increasing wait time, through use of journals and other written forms in advance of oral discussion, and by allowing students to work out responses in small groups. Fordham (2006) describes the responses of teachers and preservice teachers who had never thought of questions as anything other than a way to assess comprehension. She suggests that appropriate questions can also encourage the cognitive behaviors, like making predictions, that teachers keep, focus on "encourage."

LEARNING TO PREDICT

1. Recast your thinking as a teacher about the purpose questions serve. Questions from the teacher may promote better inferences, good predictions, and more transfer of knowledge to new situations in addition to their role as a check for comprehension or for other assessment purposes.

2. Increase the opportunities for students to think through and respond thoughtfully to the questions they encounter in the classroom.

3. Ensure that students are taught how to ask questions that further their thinking about classroom content and about how they learn best.

4. Model responses to questions that show students how to construct the response required. Don't forget that questions often look forward through content to reducing uncertainty about the content and predicting what may happen next or what the structure of the text may next suggest.

5. Consider the questions at the end of the textbook chapter as useful tools that can foster discussion, provoke thoughtful responses, and expand what students know about the topics in the chapter. We contend that when these textbook questions are useful, it is because the focus is on the construction of knowledge rather than on obtaining one-dimensional responses that might be construed as correct by the teacher. Knowledge sometimes is not as immutable

as we think; questions about text can promote inquiry and an understanding of how knowledge is constructed.

6. Use questions orally, in writing, in small groups, with individuals, and with the whole class to prompt thinking before students read, during reading to guide readers who are novices in the field of inquiry, and after reading to extend thinking and to assess what students know.

APPLICATIONS AND EXAMPLES

Secondary Classroom.   High school students reading *The Good Earth* (Buck, 1931) must make sense of another culture and a trying time in the life of a family where the situation the characters confront, on the surface, is beyond the scope of any they have experienced. Notice how teacher Cheryl Wegener uses questions to help students understand the novel and the situations confronting the characters rather than simply assessing what they know about the plot, characters, or theme (Table 9.1).

IN HER OWN WORDS: Cheryl Wegener, Eastern Michigan Writing Project, Brighton High School, Brighton, Michigan

After reading a chapter of text where the main character of O-lan kills her daughter shortly after its birth, students are sometimes confused. Was the baby stillborn? Did it die of natural causes shortly after its birth? Did O-lan really kill it? What is going through Wang Lung's mind (the father) as he buries the baby, all the while knowing that the mongrel dog lurks nearby and will immediately consume the corpse after it leaves? Outrage commonly follows these questions, leading to a discussion where many morals and dilemmas are examined. Students are presented with a series of dilemmas that are based on concepts from the novel. Students begin thinking about the dilemma presented and the follow-up questions by first responding in journals. This is followed by small group discussions, allowing students to share ideas and different points of views. Students also reflect upon how the perceptions, beliefs, and values influence the way they make decisions.

One strategy requires the students to step into the shoes of the character forced to make the decision and examine it through their eyes. Using key questions, students had to understand the text on multiple levels in order to fully respond.

"They needed to demonstrate not only basic knowledge about the text but also higher levels of understanding about characterization, plot, and theme" (Friedman, 2000, p. 101). The use of a Dilemma Worksheet (Table 9.1) helps to facilitate this process. After examining this section of text, students are asked to predict the future of the Lung family. Will they survive the famine? Will they be forced to sell the daughter known as the Poor Fool? In order to make such predictions, students may need clarification regarding the social norms in regards to the selling of daughters. They will also need to understand the hierarchy of the time, and what that meant to the Lung family.

Table 9.1   Dilemma Worksheet

What is O-lan's dilemma?

What are the two possible choices of the dilemma?

Choice 1

Choice 2

What information, evidence, or expertise does O-lan have to support her first choice?

What information, evidence, or expertise does O-lan have to support her second choice?

Evaluate her final decision and action. How does O-lan justify her decision? What information and evidence does she consider in her justification? Can O-lan ever be certain that she made the best decision?

Based on your values, beliefs, opinion, evidence, or other information, do you believe that O-lan made the best decision? Why or why not?

Elementary Classroom.   *Bud, Not Buddy* (Curtis, 2002) provides Marla Green with many opportunities to use questions with her students. She employs questions before students read that help them learn about the setting of the novel and she asks questions—and encourages students to ask questions—as the novel unfolds. These set the stage for more thinking later.

IN HER OWN WORDS: Marla Green, Kelso School District, Kelso, Washington

I realize some students won't have the schemata to attach new learning if it's not pre-taught. Consider little things like, "What food was available in the 1930s? Were there restaurants? Did they have a McDonalds?" It seems silly, but some kids really wouldn't have a clue. In chapter two, an altercation arises. Mrs. Amos walks in on Todd beating the heck out of Bud. At this point, I plan to ask for predictions, calling for questions at the interpretive level. Questions like, "What do you think is going to happen next? Will Todd get into trouble or will it be the 'foster kid,' Bud, who gets the short end of the stick? What would you do if you were Mrs. Amos?" These questions will give the students an opportunity to form their own opinions and prepare them for further discussion after reading.

10 Making Connections

Earlier (see cognitive student strategies 5 and 6), we explored how background and prior knowledge are critical if students are to make sense of the new material they encounter. In those strategy descriptions, we emphasized what students and teachers can do before reading a text to either build appropriate new knowledge or to activate the background and prior knowledge that will be relevant. However, background and prior knowledge play key roles in understanding texts in other ways: intertextuality, the types of connections they make, and the literary experience the connections offer students.

Intertextuality.   In modern use, *intertextuality* encompasses a variety of other, more nuanced, terms. When one text shapes or informs the direction, tone, style, or meaning of another, we have intertextuality. Allusion and parody are two forms of intertextuality where an author connects, borrows, transforms, or imports elements from another text. However, the term is not limited to what authors do with their written work in relation to other works. A reader, working with a text, may also connect patterns, themes, and characterizations from other sources read or encountered previously. Intertextuality has been called a dialogue among texts (Foster, 2003) and our use of that phrase is a form of intertextuality. In fact, making connections is rewarding; let's connect this text with Foster's text directly: "The basic premise of intertextuality is really pretty simple: everything's connected. In other words, anything you write is connected to other written things" (p. 189). Whether the source is cited (as convention dictates we should in this type of writing) or the source is Shakespeare, a religious text, or a movie that your students went to see last weekend, noticing and making connections between texts enriches the experience for every reader.

Types of Connections.   Here, we borrow from the work of Harvey and Goudvis (2000) whose strategies include teaching students to make connections of three types. In text-to-self connections, students are encouraged to think about the background knowledge they have about their own lives and experiences and connect that with the texts they read. Text-to-text connections are the sort of connections readers make and that we discussed in the previous paragraph about intertextuality. Text-to-world connections ask readers to notice the similarities and relationships between the background knowledge they have about the world and how it works with the text before them. Harvey and Goudvis caution teachers and readers about tangential connections that do little to advance understanding of the text. Making connections is fun, of course, but the connections a reader makes today create tomorrow's existing (prior knowledge and background knowledge) knowledge which enriches future reading with additional connections. Students who make connections between and among themselves, their world, and the texts they encounter know how to pay attention to the attributes of each that make prediction possible.

Literary Experience.   Teachers of literature often need students to notice the connection between the literature at hand and the literature from another time (last week, last year, two millenniums ago). It is tempting to expect students, who may have read the source text, to simply make the connection between source text and current text. Sometimes, they can't. Our students are competent novices; they notice what we point out and tentatively make connections of their own. Making connections is a kind of risk; you likely remember raising your hand and saying something like, "This story kind of reminds me of another one I recently read." But when pushed to say why, it became difficult. Connections take time, and the attributes of the connectors aren't always readily apparent. The more connections a reader can recognize, even with prompting from the teacher or text itself, the more the reader will be able to make connections solo. That's just how connections work—it's exponential—so patience with students who don't see what we see as experts in our disciplines is an important key to helping students take the risks associated with trying out a new connection.

LEARNING TO PREDICT

1. Daniels (1994) offers eight prompts for connecting a text to self, other texts, and the world. Connect reading to
   a. your own life
   b. happenings at school or in your neighborhood
   c. similar events at other times and places
   d. other people or problems
   e. other books or stories
   f. other writings on the same topic
   g. other writing by the same author
   h. things the reading just reminds you of

2. Teach students to think about whether a connection is useful in constructing meaning about the text at hand or if it is just tangential or superficial. Modeling how to tell the difference is a sound instructional practice.

3. Offer students the opportunity to read texts that are exportable. Smith and Wilhelm (2002) found that young men in high school like to read things they can talk about or export into a conversation. They offer the example of a student who read the *Wall Street Journal* with the intention of using that as a foundation for discussion with his father. Exportable text, while often easily captured and reduced to headlines, main ideas, and sound bites, offer students the chance to think of themselves as literate and to make connections as a result of the conversation. Modeling, again, is a sound technique, but be certain to tell students what you are doing and why.

4. Be patient and point out connections you see as a teacher. Ask students to elaborate or build on those. Patterns detected from past encounters with text invariably translate to predictions during encounters with new texts. Did you see the movie where the stranger rides into town, but the townsfolk are in trouble? Even if you didn't see it yet, we bet you know how it turns out.

APPLICATIONS AND EXAMPLES

Secondary Classroom.   Eric was assigned the role of "connector" for the discussion in his literature circle group (Daniels, 1994), but he did not know what to do. The book his group had chosen to read was *The Young Man and the Sea* by Rodman Philbrick (2004). You have probably already guessed that the book is built along the lines of Hemingway's *The Old Man and the Sea* (1952). In Philbrick's book, the narrator is Skiff Beaman. Skiff's mother has died, his father has given up on much of life, his father's boat has sunk at the dock, and the town bully makes fun of Skiff all the time.

"Mr. Wolsey, I have no idea what connections to make for discussion tomorrow. I get that the story is about a big fish and a boat like Santiago from the old man book. But what else is there?"

"Okay, that's a pretty good start. You noticed that this book is a lot like the book we read together in class last month. Is Skiff at all like you in any way?"

"No way," he said. "My dad sells cars and works hard, mom works at a school and isn't anywhere close to dead. No one at school makes fun of me, so no connection there."

"You're right, there's not much to work with on that score. Let's try something else. We read *The Outsiders* (Hinton, 1967) at the beginning of the year. Do you remember how Ponyboy and Johnny felt when they had to live in the abandoned church by themselves?"

"Yeah, sure, they were pretty lonely. Not only did the socs cut them out of everything or beat them up, their own friends didn't know where they were."

"They were pretty lonely. Hmmm."

"Oh, I get it. Skiff must be lonely, too. I need to get this in my journal before discussion tomorrow."

Eighth-grade students in Mrs. Jones' class are also learning to clarify difficult passages and make connections through reading of "The Raven," by Edgar Allan Poe. She stops at key points to ask students for predictions and clarifies points where she can connect her knowledge of Greek mythology with that of the poem.

IN HER OWN WORDS: Karen Jones, Nashville Christian School, Nashville, Tennessee

After reading stanzas seven and eight in which the Raven is introduced, students make predictions and we clarify connections to other texts and world knowledge.

> Open here I flung the shutter, when, with many a flirt and flutter,
> In there stepped a stately Raven of the saintly days of yore;
> Not the least obeisance made he; not a minute stopped or stayed he;
> But with mien of lord or lady, perched above my chamber door—
> Perched upon a bust of Pallas, just above my chamber door—
> Perched, and sat, and nothing more.
> Then this ebony bird beguiling my sad fancy into smiling,
> By the grave and stern decorum of the countenance it wore,
> "Though thy crest be shorn and shaven, thou," I said, "art sure no craven,
> Ghastly, grim and ancient Raven wandering from the Nightly shore—
> Tell me what thy lordly name is on the Night's Plutonian shore!"
> Quoth the Raven, "Nevermore"

From "The Raven," by Edgar Allan Poe

After some discussion, the students will probably arrive at the following clarifications on their own:

1. The Raven is a metaphor for the lost Lenore.
2. The Raven represents a messenger from the after-life.

However, the phrase "perched upon a bust of Pallas just above my chamber door—" leaves the students a bit confused, so I ask them, "Why would the speaker have a bust of

Pallas in his chamber?" One student will probably ask who Pallas is, but if not, I will ask students if they know who this is. After taking responses, I will then clarify to students that Pallas is a pseudonym for Athena. Students will think of one question dealing with possible connections between Pallas/Athena, the Raven, the speaker, and Lenore, and I will ask them to write it down in their journals.

Elementary Classroom.   In their partner discussions during the read-aloud of the *Olivia* books (e.g., Falconer, 2000), the students in Mr. Castagnera's first-grade class focused on what might happen to their favorite character. To help them figure out what might happen, Mr. Castagnera focused on making connections. As he said to his students, "When you can make a connection, you think like the character and then you might be able to figure out what will happen. Of course, some authors like to be tricky and they give us clues that throw us off. But that's okay, making predictions helps us learn and remember, regardless if we're right, right?" Heads nod as the students wait excitedly for their teacher to start reading.

On the first page, Jacob says to Mariah, "I'm good at a lot of things, too. I bet Olivia is good at art because I am good at drawing things I do good."

Later, when it's Mariah's turn, she says, "I saw this show on TV, she had to change all of the time because she was scared. I think Olivia is scared because she's changing her clothes too many times. She's probably scared that she's going to get in trouble."

11 Summarizing

Quick! Summarize an article you read from the morning newspaper. Be careful; this is trickier than it appears. To complete this task, you might return to the article, reread it, and identify only the most important points. If you take this approach, you are summarizing. Another approach is to attempt to recall the article from memory. If you take this approach, you are no longer summarizing; instead, you are retelling. Retelling and summarizing are not the same thing exactly, and are often confused for each other. In retelling, important points may be lost among all the details or may not be recalled at all. Retelling does have an important role to play in classrooms that value literacy. Moss (2004) points out that retelling is an important technique that teachers can use to understand what students know about stories they read, and they lead to better summarizing.

In summarizing, students must pay attention to the most relevant attributes of a text passage and determine which are most significant in relation to the rest of the text, the writer's purpose, and the reader's needs. Summarizing and predicting share the characteristic of requiring the thinker to identify important attributes from among significant and less significant details. Students who stop to summarize what they read are also more likely to notice the elements of the text that lead to better predictions as they work through the text.

Summarizing means making judgments about what is relatively important and what is not. The structure of the source text tends to help students organize their summaries, and with texts that are poorly organized the student summarizer must compensate by reordering concepts (Kintsch, 1990) so they make sense in the final product. The ability to reformulate text to produce more sophisticated generalizations also appears to increase as students become older. Of note for teachers: Training in how to summarize has positive and measurable effects, as a study of seventh graders found (Rinehart, Stahl, & Erickson, 1986). The implication for teachers is that a student who could effectively summarize in fifth grade may need more practice and additional instruction in the eleventh grade.

LEARNING TO PREDICT

1. Teach students the difference between retelling and summarizing and let them know that both are important cognitive skills. Summaries can be drawn from accurate retellings.

2. Provide models of well-crafted summaries, written and oral, using source texts students have read. Ask students to work with partners and in small groups to refine their summaries. By comparing the work of others who have read the same material, students can compare the quality of their summarizations and learn from the transaction.

3. Students can create summaries in stages as they work with manageable chunks of larger texts (Hidi & Anderson, 1986). These summaries may be combined and revisited. Note-taking structures often incorporate summarizing (e.g., Callison, 2003).

4. Provide time for students to reread and use notes and other written summaries as a basis for discussion and responding to texts. Ask students to use their summaries to predict what comes later in longer texts and to connect what they know from other sources.

APPLICATIONS AND EXAMPLES

Elementary Classroom.   Ms. Roberta Donahue is convinced that summaries are an important part of predicting. She is so convinced of this that she has her fourth-grade students summarize newspaper articles several times per week. She models good summary sentences and the class constructs several summaries together during the beginning of the year. When she believes that they are ready, she asks members of the class to hone their summarizing skills at least three times per week. Students cut interesting newspaper articles out and then attach summaries of them. Ms. Donahue reviews these in a reader/writer conference with each student as they focus on the main ideas, supporting details, and how the summaries help readers pay attention to critical information. Ms. Donahue also notes "summary writing serves several purposes. It aids in their prediction skills as well as their writing skills. Over time, and with practice summarizing, my students write stronger papers. They know what's important, what they want to say and how to support their arguments with details."

Secondary Classroom.   Jennifer Horvath scaffolds instruction such that students understand the concept of summarizing before moving on to more difficult texts.

IN HER OWN WORDS: Jennifer Horvath, Mariner High School, Cape Coral, Florida

This lesson is organized to teach students how to summarize and find the main idea of a piece of literature. I have designed this lesson for my ninth- to eleventh-grade intensive reading students. I have modified this lesson to meet the needs of students with learning disabilities by modeling the process of summarizing and finding a main idea with them. My intensive reading classes are filled with many struggling readers. Most of the students are just a little below grade level and need extra practice reading to help them catch up, but I also have several students with different types of learning disabilities (LD). The students that I teach are able to function normally with the rest of the class but usually need "explicit modeling and explicit practice" as mentioned in the article by Gore (2004, p. 97). The lesson on summarizing will reinforce the skill for all of the students while also giving extra support to some students. I have incorporated a graphic organizer into this lesson by having the students complete the following simple five question graphic organizer.

Who?	What?	Where?	When?	Why?	How?

When Karen Jones' eighth-grade students learn about devices in poetry, they begin by ensuring that they understand the main ideas of the poem through summarizing. In this case, students are reading "The Raven" by Edgar Allan Poe and using summarizing tools to complete their assignment (Figures 11.1a and 11.1b).

Figure 11.1a

Summary Strategy: Using a graphic organizer. (Ask students to complete the following steps.)

1. Think of a time when you lost someone or something very important to you.
2. Reread the poem, and then think about how the speaker's experience compares and contrasts to your own.
3. Write about the poem. In the first column, describe your experience and the feelings you have about it. In the second column, write about the speaker's loss and summarize his feelings as the poet expressed them. In the bottom section, summarize your idea of who or what the raven represents and explain why you came to that conclusion.

Figure 11.1b

Name: _____

SUMMARY ORGANIZER

My experience:	Character's experience:

My summary/resolution statement:

⟨⟨⟩⟩   ***IN HER OWN WORDS:* Karen Jones, Nashville Christian School, Nashville, Tennessee**

In this lesson I show how those strategies are incorporated. The lesson begins by displaying an overhead with examples of newspaper headlines and lead summaries. I will then discuss with the students what type of information is given to the reader in these items. Next, I will put up an overhead and take the students through each step of creating a summary and then from the summary create a main idea. I use the nursery rhyme "Jack and Jill" to model this process for the students. Once the class and I have completed the first summary together, I place the students in groups of three and have them complete the same assignment using a random nursery rhyme that I have provided for them. When the students are finished, we come back together as a class and the students volunteer to read their rhyme, headline, and summary to the rest of the students.

12 Visualizing

In cognitive student strategy 4, Jason Lefevre told us about an elegant fishing story, *A River Runs Through It* (Maclean, 1976). In that novella, the author describes the Big Blackfoot River:

> The straight line on the map also suggests its glacial origins; it has no meandering valley, and its few farms are mostly on its southern tributaries which were not ripped up by the glaciers; instead of opening into a wide flood plain near its mouth, the valley, which was cut overnight by a disappearing lake when the great ice dam melted, gets narrower and narrower until the only way a river, an old logging railroad, and an automobile road can fit into it is for two of them to take to the mountainsides. (p. 13)

Now, close your eyes. We're going to summarize.

Summarize, with our eyes closed, you ask? Of course, we are going to summarize visually. With your eyes closed (we know—you're peeking in order to read these words), imagine the Big Blackfoot River as the narrator of Maclean's story described it. Can you picture a mountain river in a valley so narrow there is almost no bank on either side; do you see and feel the water rushing through the gorge? If you can see this river, then you have an idea about where much of the rest of the story takes place, and you will be able to use that information to make predictions about events in the story. When we visualize, we are summarizing but not with words. The pictures we imagine when we read help us think about and reconceptualize the information in the text we have read.

Ten fourth-grade students worked with teacher Linda Parsons (2006) to think about what visualization tools they used as they read and how they engaged with texts. These fourth graders identified three dimensions of visualizing as they read: picturing, watching, and seeing. "Picturing" did not involve movement. In the previous passage, you probably visualized a still image of the river, as if your construction of the image was a photograph or drawing. "Watching" involved the young readers thinking of themselves as being in the story but unable to interact in it. The students characterized this as the story occurring "in front of you" (p. 497) and the action is outside of the reader. Readers who visualized themselves as being participants in the story or who feel they are experiencing it were "seeing." All of these dimensions were useful, and students proficient at visualizing moved fluidly from one type of visualizing to another as the story progressed. As they do so, they pay attention to relevant attributes of the story that help them construct the visual and that allow them to reduce uncertainty through increasingly fine predictions.

Besides the visualizations that are mental constructions of what is not physically present, student readers also learn from the visuals that accompany some texts and they learn to create their own visuals digitally or on paper for others to see. Smolkin and Donovan (2005) suggest that teachers should direct students' attention to visuals that accompany texts and point out the connections. Teachers may also direct students' attention to specific features of the visual itself. Pointing to a map, a teacher may say, "Do you see this dotted line? It shows boundaries of the Louisiana Purchase. You will notice that it roughly matches several geographic features like the Mississippi River on the eastern side." Further, when students learn to create their own visuals for others to see, they form deeper connections to the material and add additional layers likely to improve recall and text processing (e.g., Rakes, Rakes, & Smith, 1995).

LEARNING TO PREDICT

1. Identify passages during shared reading, guided reading, or read-alouds where you can pause and ask students to visualize the scene, character, event, or condition.

2. Provide opportunities for students to draw their visualizations of stories and nonfiction texts.

3. Point out the visuals that the publisher or author includes with text. Identify how the visual enhances understanding of the textual material and what parts of the visual may require extra scrutiny.

APPLICATIONS AND EXAMPLES

Elementary Classroom.   Jeri Sorensen asks her kindergarten through second-grade students to visualize and draw as a means to check comprehension.

 IN HER OWN WORDS: Jeri Sorensen, Mary B. Lewis Elementary School, Bloomington, California

I teach English language learners at the earliest levels of their development in Bloomington, California. The students are in kindergarten through second grade. Recently, students were working on several themes depending on grade level. Kindergarten was learning about seasons, first grade worked on a unit about the farm, and second grade worked on a theme called "From Field to Table." I wanted to check the students' comprehension of material that was read to them, so I chose poetry as the genre. The poem was a haiku I wrote about autumn:

> Red, orange, yellow, brown
> Falling gently to the ground,
> Twirling, whirling leaves.

I gave each student a piece of paper and some crayons, then asked them to close their eyes and listen to the poem. I told them to make a picture in their heads, then draw that picture on the paper. The kindergarten student in the group, Allison, drew a line of leaves while the first grader, Kallie, drew circles around her leaves to show that they were spinning or twirling. The pictures showed that the students understood the words in the poem. Their descriptions of their drawings showed me a glimpse of where their oral abilities in English were, as well.

I used the same procedure in a third-grade, regular education classroom of 20 students using a poem about a tree, but the poem did not include the word *tree*. Rather, it described a tree. After reading this poem, I again asked students to draw the picture they saw in their minds and to write a sentence to tell me about their pictures (Figures 12.1a and 12.1b).

Figure 12.1a Myna's Illustration

Figure 12.1b Myna's Sentences

There is two grils looking at the tree. There is wind Blowing. There is lots of wind.

13 Asking and Making Clarifications

Clarification requires readers to recall earlier predictions and points of confusion in critical evaluation of what the reader has encountered (Palincsar & Brown, 1984). Students might think of clarification as a refining process by which understanding is enhanced. To make a clarification, the reader must recall an earlier prediction (or a point of confusion) and determine which of the following apply:

1. The prediction was accurate.
2. The prediction was not accurate, which suggests that the reader has adjusted a construction of the text or its meaning.
3. The prediction's accuracy is still to be determined, but more information has been gained to inform or refine the prediction.

LEARNING TO PREDICT

1. As with other strategies, modeling by the teacher or capable others is a key for students to learn how clarifications are made.
2. Clarifications can be at the focal level as students use context cues to construct word meanings, recognize connecting words to understand how sentences relate to each other, and note how events lead from one to another. Clarifications at the global level about the overall themes of a story or main ideas in nonfiction also require modeling. In other words, a student who is proficient at clarifying word meanings from context may not be proficient at clarifying how one story event connects with another. The types of clarifications students are expected to make should be taught.
3. Students need practice with clarifying, as with other cognitive tasks. Consciously thinking about clarifications leads to even better clarifications and predictions.
4. To record their predictions and points of confusion, students might be encouraged to use sticky notes to flag and record exactly where in the text the thought occurred. Hashey and Connors (2003) found that students became more comfortable when they compared the concepts and vocabulary flagged with one another. The clarifications students generated when they processed their predictions and confusing points as a class were more authentic.

APPLICATIONS AND EXAMPLES

Secondary Classroom.   Students reading *Call of the Wild* (London, 1915) in Mr. Wolsey's class discussed the theme in small groups. As they discussed the events of the novel, they became increasingly confused about how the events of the story were related. A prediction they had agreed upon earlier in their reading was that Buck would end his days side by side with his human friend, John Thornton. Why did Buck end up as the leader of a wolf pack?

What was the author's point after finding friendship with a Thornton? As the students struggled with the places Buck had been and where he ended up, Mr. Wolsey listened.

He thought that the text structure as outlined in the chapter titles might be helpful to them. First, he reminded them of a movie character, Luke Skywalker, who seemed to have very little to do with Buck, at first. Students remembered that Luke, as of a hero, was similar to another hero they had recently read about, Beowulf. Then, he pointed out the chapter titles. In short order, they noticed the pattern, the heroic cycle, lent meaning to the story. Like Skywalker and Beowulf, Buck had been on the hero's journey (Campbell, 1968), an archetype that helped them understand that Buck's journey returned him to his primitive home among the wolves. By pointing out the text structure at the point in the discussion when the students most needed it and reminding them of prior knowledge they already had available, the students were able to make global clarifications about the theme of a novel that had previously left them confused.

Elementary Classroom   Toni Kinsey's sixth graders make predictions and clarify as they read about Michigan's northern neighbor, Canada.

 IN HER OWN WORDS: Toni Kinsey, South Meadows School, Chelsea, Michigan

In the section about European immigrants, students look at the picture of the French and Indian War prior to reading and see the suffering of the British. Without reading the selection, students may predict that the French and people of the First Nations won the battle. Another prediction that students often make is that the areas in which most Canadians live are in the Southern regions. By looking at the map of geographic features, students are able to predict the settlement areas prior to reading the section entitled, "Where do most Canadians live?" Further they may predict that the rugged terrain and cold climate in the North makes the newest territory, gained in 1999 by the Inuit, Nunavut, less habitable. Each of these predictions will become important to discussions later in the unit.

As they read, students need clarification about the reasons Canada is a multilingual and multicultural country. Students often accidentally call the English language, "American." They frequently see people conform and become part of a homogeneous group. Middle school students fear being different and may forget the importance of cultural differences and traditions. I model clarification by referring students to the examples of many different cultures found in the textbook then discussing the many contributions each culture has made to our own and the notion of valuing differences. In order to find more information, I model and have students glance through the book locating the "Spotlight on Culture" boxes. By looking at these, students will see the unique traits of many different cultures. We will discuss the notion of living in harmony as opposed to conforming.

REFERENCES

Allbritton, D. (2004). Strategic production of predictive inferences during comprehension. *Discourse Processes, 38*, 309–322.

Alvermann, D. E., & Phelps, S. (2005). *Content reading and literacy: Succeeding in today's classrooms* (4th ed.). Boston: Pearson Education.

Anderson, R. C. (2004). Role of the reader's schema in comprehension, learning, and memory. In R. B. Ruddell & N. J. Unrau (Eds.), *Theoretical models and processes of reading* (5th ed., pp. 594–606). Newark, DE: International Reading Association.

Ashley, C. W. (1944). *The Ashley book of knots.* Garden City, NY: Doubleday and Company, Inc.

Baumann, J. F., Edwards, E. C., Boland, E. M., Olejnik, S., & Kame'enui, E. J. (2003). Vocabulary tricks: Effects of instruction in morphology and context on fifth-grade students' ability to derive and infer word meanings. *American Educational Research Journal, 40*, 447–494.

Betts, E. A. (1946). *Foundations of reading instruction with emphasis on differentiated guidance.* New York: American Book Company.

Bourke, L. (1991). *Eye spy: A mysterious alphabet.* New York: Trumpet Club and Chronicle Books.

Bowyer-Crane, C., & Snowling, M. J. (2005). Assessing children's inference generation: What do tests of reading comprehension measure? *British Journal of Educational Psychology, 75*, 189–201.

Bransford, J. D., Brown, A. L., & Cocking, R. R. (Eds.). (2000). *How people learn: Brain, mind, experience, and school.* Washington, DC: National Academy Press. Available: http://newton.nap.edu/html/howpeople1/ch3.html

Buck, P. S. (1931). *The good earth.* New York: Washington Square Press.

Burmark, L. (2002). *Visual literacy: Learn to see, see to learn.* Alexandria, VA: Association for Supervision and Curriculum Development.

Cain, K., Oakhill, J., & Bryant, P. (2004). Children's reading comprehension ability: Concurrent prediction by working memory, verbal ability, and component skills. *Journal of Educational Psychology, 96*, 31–42.

Callison, D. (2003). Note-taking: Different notes for different research stages. *School Library Media Activities Monthly, 19*(7), 33–45.

Campbell, J. (1968). *The hero with a thousand faces* (2nd ed.). Princeton, NJ: Princeton University Press.

Chapman, C., & King, R. (2003). *Differentiated instruction: Strategies for reading in the content areas.* Thousand Oaks, CA: Corwin Press.

Curtis, C. P. (2002). *Bud, not Buddy.* New York: Doubleday Dell Publishing Group.

Daines, D. (1986). Are teachers asking higher level questions? *Education, 106*, 368–374.

Daniels, H. (1994). *Literature circles: Voice and choice in the student-centered classroom.* York, ME: Stenhouse.

Daniels, H. (2002). *Literature circles: Voice and choice in book clubs and reading groups.* York, ME: Stenhouse.

Dechant, E. (1991). *Understanding and teaching reading: An interactive model.* Hillsdale, NJ: Lawrence Erlbaum Associates.

Devine, T. G., & Kania, J. S. (2003). Studying: Skills, strategies, and systems. In J. Flood, D. Lapp, J. R. Squire, & J. M. Jensen (Eds.), *Handbook of research on teaching the English language arts* (2nd ed., pp. 942–954). Mahwah, NJ: Lawrence Erlbaum Associates.

Dymock, S. (2005). Teaching expository text structure awareness. *The Reading Teacher, 59,* 177–182.

Ehri, L. (1995). Phases of development in learning to read words by sight. *Journal of Research in Reading, 18,* 116–125.

Ehri, L., & McCormick, S. (2004). Phases of word learning: Implications for instruction with delayed and disabled readers. In R. B. Ruddell & N. J. Unrau (Eds.), *Theoretical models and processes of reading* (5th ed., pp. 365–389). Newark, DE: International Reading Association.

Falconer, I. (2000). *Olivia.* New York: Atheneum Books for Young Readers.

Feathers, K. M. (1993). *Infotext: Reading and learning.* Scarborough, Ontario: Pippin Publishing.

Fisher, D., Brozo, W., Frey, N., & Ivey, G. (2007). *Fifty content area strategies for adolescent literacy.* Upper Saddle River, NJ: Pearson, Merrill, Prentice Hall.

Fordham, N. W. (2006). Crafting questions that address comprehension strategies in content reading. *The Journal of Adolescent and Adult Literacy, 49,* 390–396.

Foster, T. C. (2003). *How to read literature like a professor: A lively and entertaining guide to reading between the lines.* New York: HarperCollins.

Frey, N., Fisher, D., & Berkin, A. (in press). *Good habits, great readers.* Upper Saddle River, NJ: Merrill Education.

Friedman, A. (2000). Nurturing reflective judgment through literature-based inquiry. *English Journal, 89,* 96–104.

Fullan, M., Hill, P., & Crévola, C. (2006). *Breakthrough.* Thousand Oaks, CA: Corwin.

Gick, M. L., & Holyoak, K. J. (1983). Schema induction and analogical transfer. *Cognitive Psychology, 15,* 1–38.

Gore, M. (2004). *Successful inclusion strategies for secondary and middle school teachers: Keys to help struggling learners access the curriculum.* Thousand Oaks, CA: Corwin Press.

Grisham, D. L., & Wolsey, T. D. (2006). Recentering the middle school classroom as a vibrant learning community: Students, literacy and technology intersect. *Journal of Adolescent and Adult Literacy, 49,* 648–660.

Harris, T. L., & Hodges, R. E. (Eds.). (1995). *The literacy dictionary: The vocabulary of reading and writing.* Newark, DE: International Reading Association.

Harvey, S., & Goudvis, A. (2000). *Strategies that work: Teaching comprehension to enhance understanding.* Portland, ME: Stenhouse.

Hashey, J. M., & Connors, D. J. (2003). Learn from our journey: Reciprocal teaching action research. *The Reading Teacher, 57,* 224–232.

Hemingway, E. (1952). *The old man and the sea.* London: Jonathan Cape.

Hemingway, E. (1987). A day's wait. *The complete short stories of Ernest Hemingway: The Finca Vigía edition* (pp. 332–334). New York: Charles Scribner's Sons.

Hidi, S., & Anderson, V. (1986). Producing written summaries: Task demands, cognitive operations, and implications for instruction. *Review of Educational Research, 56,* 473–493.

Hinton, S. E. (1967). *The outsiders.* New York: Dell.

Holman, C. H., & Harmon, W. (1992). *A handbook to literature* (6th ed.). New York: Macmillan Publishing Co.

Holyoak, K. J., & Thagard, P. (1995). *Mental leaps: Analogy in creative thought.* Cambridge, MA: The MIT Press.

Innocenti, R. (1985). *Rose Blanche.* Mankato, MN: Creative Editions.

Kintsch, E. (1990). Macroprocesses and microprocesses in the development of summarization skill. *Cognition and Instruction, 7*, 161–195.

Kragler, S., Walker, C. A., & Martin, L. E. (2005). Strategy instruction in primary content textbooks. *The Reading Teacher, 59*, 254–261.

Kramer, S. (1992). *Lightning.* Minneapolis, MN: Carolrhoda Books.

Liben, D., & Liben, M. (2005). Learning to read in order to learn: Building a program for upper-elementary students. *Phi Delta Kappan, 86*, 401–406.

London, J. (1915). *Call of the wild.* New York: Grosset & Dunlap.

Maclean, N.(1976). *A river runs through it.* Chicago, IL: The University of Chicago Press.

Malcolm X. (1997). Hair. In C. B. Divakaruni (Ed.), *Multitudes: Cross-cultural readings for writers* (pp. 327–329). New York: McGraw-Hill.

McGee, A., & Johnson, H. (2003). The effect of inference training on skilled and less skilled comprehenders. *Educational Psychology, 23*, 49–59.

Moore, P. J., & Scevak, J. J. (1997). Learning from texts and visual aids: A developmental perspective. *Journal of Research in Reading, 20*, 205–223.

Moss, B. (2004). Teaching expository text structures through information trade book retellings. *The Reading Teacher, 57*, 710–718.

Palincsar, A. S., & Brown, A. L. (1984). Reciprocal teaching of comprehension-fostering and comprehension-monitoring activities. *Cognition and Instruction, 1*, 117–175.

Parsons, L. (2006). Visualizing worlds from words on a page. *Language Arts, 83*, 492–500.

Philbrick, R. (2004). *The young man and the sea.* New York: Scholastic.

Rakes, G. C., Rakes, T. A., & Smith, L. J. (1995). Using visuals to enhance secondary students' reading comprehension of expository texts. *Journal of Adolescent and Adult Literacy, 39*, 46–54.

Richards, J. C., & Anderson, N. A. (2003). How do you know? A strategy to help emergent readers make inferences. *The Reading Teacher, 57*, 290–293.

Rinehart, S. D., Stahl, S. A., & Erickson, L. G. (1986). Some effects of summarization training on reading and studying. *Reading Research Quarterly, 21*, 422–438.

Rule, A. C., & Furletti, C. (2004). Using form and function analogy object boxes to teach human body systems. *School Science and Mathematics, 104*(4), 155–169.

Ryder, R. J., & Graves, M. (2003). *Reading and learning in the content areas* (3rd ed.). New York: John Wiley & Sons, Inc.

Smith, F. (2004). *Understanding reading* (6th ed.). Mahwah, NJ: Lawrence Erlbaum Associates.

Smith, M. W., & Wilhelm, J. D. (2002). *Reading don't fix no Chevy's.* Portsmouth, NH: Heinemann.

Smolkin, L. B., & Donovan, C. A. (2005). Looking closely at a science trade book: Gail Gibbons and multimodal literacy. *Language Arts, 83*, 52–63.

Strangman, N., & Hall, T. (2004). *Background knowledge.* Wakefield, MA: National Center on Accessing the General Curriculum. Retrieved October 6, 2006, from http://www.cast.org/publications/ncac/ncac_backknowledge.html

Tompkins, G. (2003). *Literacy for the twenty-first century* (3rd ed.). Upper Saddle River, NJ: Merrill Prentice Hall.

Trelease, J. (1982). *The read-aloud handbook.* New York: Penguin.

Trelease, J. (2006). *The read-aloud handbook* (6th ed.). New York: Penguin.

Turner, T. N. (1983). Questioning techniques: Probing for greater meaning. In J. E. Alexander (Ed.), *Teaching reading* (2nd ed., pp. 198–219). Boston: Little, Brown & Company.

Vacca, R. T., & Vacca, J. L. (2005). *Content area reading: Literacy and learning across the curriculum* (8th ed.). Boston: Pearson Education.

Wallner, J. (1987). *City mouse-country mouse and two more mouse tales from Aesop.* New York: Scholastic.

White, T. H. (1958). *The once and future king.* New York: G. P. Putnam's Sons.

Wolsey, T. D. (2004, January/February). Literature discussion in cyberspace: Young adolescents using threaded discussion groups to talk about books. *Reading Online, 7*(4). Available: http://www.readingonline.org/articles/art_index.asp?HREF=wolsey/index.html

For Twilight Zone (incomplete refs): Thompson, E., et al.

Hayes, D. (Director). (1958). Eye of the beholder [Television series episode]. In *The Twilight Zone.*

III

Instructional Routines That Promote Prediction

In the previous part, we explored some of the cognitive strategies that students might employ as they work toward making increasingly useful predictions in their reading. In addition, some examples of what teachers often do to encourage that cognitive activity were presented. Now, we turn our attention to the specific instructional routines that teachers can use in an effort to encourage the sort of cognitive activity that characterizes good thinking while students are engaged in literacy tasks.

At several points in this book, we have encouraged you to continue doing what we are confident you have always done; that is, make conscious and precise decisions about teaching methodologies and classroom structures that promote good thinking and improved ability when a literacy task is encountered. Sharing those philosophies or approaches with other teachers or administrators can inform the choices about which cognitive strategies or instructional routines might best be used universally and transparently throughout a school's curriculum (e.g., Fisher, Frey, & Williams, 2002). However, overwhelming your teaching colleagues or students with an extensive list of instructional routines and cognitive strategies is unlikely to produce a desired result. Therefore, our first challenge is initiate a dialogue with your colleagues about which routines might be most beneficial for the specific student population sitting in your classroom.

❧ INSTRUCTIONAL ROUTINES

In our work on this book, we have followed the advice of others who have carefully chosen words that convey precisely (there's that word, again) the meaning intended. Ross and McDaniel (2004) draw a distinction between the cognitive strategies that teachers expect students to employ and the instructional strategies that teachers employ to encourage cognitive activity on the part of students. For example, a teacher might use an instructional activity known widely as know–want to know–learn (KWL) (Ogle, 1986) to enhance a lesson that calls for activating background and prior knowledge (a cognitive strategy students should use in order to make sense of reading). So, in this part of the book, we will use the term *instructional routines* to characterize the tools and techniques that teachers use to encourage cognitive strategies on the part of students. In part II, we used the term *strategy* to refer to the cognitive activities expected of students. While we believe that using the term *strategy* to refer to both instructional routines and cognitive activity is all right, it is equally important to know exactly what is meant, to know exactly what the distinctions may be, when using the term. For that reason, we have used two different terms in this book.

☙ INSTRUCTIONAL ROUTINES THAT ARE EVIDENCE-BASED

Our second challenge is for you to think about which strategies and routines fit with your students' needs and which might be most beneficial to students in other classrooms. The second challenge is fairly straightforward, if not a bit more difficult to implement. In current educational parlance, the terms *research-based* and *evidence-based* are used with increasing frequency. Both terms are used to describe instructional routines teachers use and the textbooks that claim to employ such routines, yet often those that employ the terms cannot state with any certainty what research supports that routine. We challenge you to become familiar enough with the research that supports using an instructional routine and where the gaps in that knowledge base exist. In other words, if you say that something is "research-based," we encourage you to be able to identify research that supports the routine and why that routine may or may not be valuable.

Theorist Neil Postman (1992) explained that a scientific theory is only scientific to the extent that it can be shown to be false; in other words, a theory that is stated in absolute terms is not a scientific theory. Applying science, Postman contended, to social institutions is problematic, at best, because such institutions are situational, bound by time and the unique experiences of the observers. Those conceptions that cannot be tested cannot be characterized as scientific. This does not mean that a conception is not true or that it cannot tell us something about the enterprise of education; it only means that the conception is not scientific—it cannot be tested. We bring this up here because sometimes teachers know "what works" and what does not. The danger, we believe, is that a theory of what works is too often generalized (Sagor, 2000) and accepted as good for all students in any instructional situation. Such a generalization is sometimes applied in ways that are not beneficial to the actual students sitting in one's classroom and justified as "research-based." To elaborate on our challenge, we think that teachers should constantly ask themselves and their colleagues which instructional routine is most appropriate for the students they serve and which cognitive strategies are most beneficial (and why they are most beneficial) to those students.

As you read the following sections of this part, ask yourself what research supports the concept, how it helps your students (or not), and what new research must be done to add to the discussion about the utility of the instructional routine. We present two routines to facilitate modeling of students' cognitive strategies, two routines that support prediction through related cognitive structures, and eight routines that promote prediction directly.

14 Shared Reading

Sharing connotes, at times, a limited amount of something which must be divided up into smaller quantities. For example, one piece of cake and two children who want dessert calls for sharing. At other times, sharing connotes an experience that is enriched when more than one person participates in it. A movie is more fun, more memorable, more entertaining when viewed with another person; context is created and there is an opportunity to contribute to a shared meaning. A community of readers is created through sharing, too.

In shared reading, the teacher reads aloud while students read along. This differs from read-alouds where the teacher reads but students only listen. (See Table 14.1 for a comparison of several reading formats teachers may employ in the classroom.) While primary-grade teachers are familiar with shared reading using big books, upper elementary and secondary teachers often use shared reading, too. Examples of texts that may not be appropriate for students to read independently or in guided reading situations include texts with a great deal of highly technical vocabulary; texts that include concepts rich in high levels of abstraction; texts for readers who have not fully integrated graphophonic, syntactic, and semantic cueing systems fluently; and texts that provide a foundation or touchstone for further study.

Shared reading provides the teacher with the opportunity to model predicting one's way through text. When a teacher stops at various points and asks students to predict word meanings or future events, the cognitive strategy of predicting is modeled for the student participants in the shared reading. We have found, as others have (e.g., Dreher, 2003; Allen 2002), that secondary students enjoy the shared reading experience just as much as first graders do. Teachers often provide older students with choices of texts to improve engagement with literacy tasks; less often teachers provide opportunities for students to choose the format of the tasks—shared reading, independent reading, read-aloud, and so forth.

STEP BY STEP

1. A text is chosen by the teacher, by the students, or through a negotiated process dependent on learning goals and desired outcomes.

2. Prereading activities are identified based on the goals and outcomes as well as students' needs. These can include a preview of vocabulary; an overview of text structures; a preview of major concepts; a preview of graphs, pictures, charts, headings, and other text features; or a picture walk. Students may make predictions based on the prereading.

3. During reading, the teacher stops to model predictions and to solicit predictions from students. Primary-grade teachers may point to the words and phrases as the reading progresses. The teacher may also stop at various points in the reading to review previous predictions about events in the story and to refine predictions as the story unfolds.

4. Students and teachers work on skills related to the reading (letter–sound correspondences, punctuation and other usage, comprehension strategies, etc.). They may also return to the text or to a similar text for rereading or independent reading. Strickland (1998) describes a strategy for situating skills instruction in meaningful literacy experiences as a whole–part–whole that starts with a whole text, explores with students parts of language and skills with language, then returns to a whole text for application and practice.

Table 14.1   Advantages and Disadvantages of the Five Types of Classroom Reading

Type	Advantages	Disadvantages
Shared Reading Teacher reads aloud while students follow along using individual copies of the book, class chart, or big book.	• Access to books students could not read themselves • Teacher models fluent reading • Opportunities to model reading strategies • Develops a community of readers	• Multiple copies, a class chart, or a big book needed. • Text may not be appropriate for all students. • Students may not be interested in the text.
Guided Reading Teacher supports students as they apply reading strategies and skills to read a text.	• Teach skills and strategies. • Teacher provides direction and scaffolding. • Opportunities to model reading strategies. • Use with unfamiliar texts.	• Multiple copies of text needed. • Teacher controls the reading experience. • Some students may not be interested in the text.
Independent Reading Students read a text on their own.	• Develops responsibility and ownership. • Self-selection of texts. • Experience is more authentic.	• Students may need assistance to read the text. • Little teacher involvement and control.
Buddy Reading Two students read or reread a text together.	• Collaboration between students. • Students assist each other. • Use to reread familiar texts. • Develops reading fluency. • Students talk and share interpretations.	• Limited teacher involvement. • Less teacher control.
Reading Aloud to Students Teacher or other fluent reader reads aloud to students	• Access to books students could not read themselves. • Reader models fluent reading. • Opportunities to model reading strategies. • Develops a community of readers. • Use when only one copy of text is available.	• No opportunity for students themselves to read. • Text may not be appropriate for all students. • Students may not be interested in the text.

Reprinted with permission from Tompkins, G. (2003). *Literacy for the 21st century* (3rd edition), p. 42.

APPLICATIONS AND EXAMPLES

Primary Classroom.   Mrs. Levick's first graders are learning to predict using *The Three Little Pigs* (Parkes, 1985), a retold version of the classic story. At the same time, they work on fluency (intonation and expression).

IN HER OWN WORDS: Susan Levick, Alice Birney Elementary School, Colton, California.

The Three Little Pigs

Materials: *The Three Little Pigs* retold by Brenda Parkes and Judith Smith, illustrated by Ester Kasepuu, big book, (1985).

Anticipatory Set: Display the big book for the class. Discuss the title, illustration on the front cover, and how a story might change when it is retold. Ask students if they are familiar with the story and make predictions about how this version might be different.

Objective: Students will participate in a shared reading, predict events, and demonstrate the appropriate expression and intonation while reading fluently.

Instruction and Modeling: Explain to the class why using the appropriate expression and intonation can make reading a book out loud more interesting. Read *The Three Little Pigs* to the class modeling the expression and intonation. Stop reading after the wolf visits each pig's house. Solicit predictions about what might happen next.

Guided Practice: Read the story again with the students joining in when reading the speaking parts of the three pigs and the wolf. Ask students to note differences between the classic version of the story and this retold version.

Check for Understanding: Clarify questions about vocabulary words and the use of expression and intonation. Monitor students for intonation and expression while rereading the story.

Independent Practice: Reread the story with individual students reading the parts of the three pigs and the wolf.

Closure: Review the objective with the class. Verbally praise students for participating in the lesson.

Secondary Classroom.   Eighth-grade students we worked with were assigned to read *The Old Man and the Sea* (Hemingway, 1952). The sentence structures and the plot in this story are not very difficult; however, this novel presents other problems for student readers who lack guidance. While most of the vocabulary is familiar, a few terms are used in unfamiliar ways—dolphin is a fish most often known as mahi mahi today, but students confuse it with the marine mammal, for example. The cause of the phosphorescent glow of the sea is unfamiliar even to Southern California students, and baseball legends of the mid-twentieth century are all but unknown to students today. The allegorical nature of the story would elude most students if the novel were assigned as independent reading in class or as homework. For this novel, shared reading is appropriate for students. In addition to prereading activities to work with concepts and vocabulary, shared reading allows the students to predict events using their background knowledge, and knowledge of story structures, literary techniques, and the events of the story.

As the reading progresses, the teacher stops at a point in the story where Santiago, the old man of the title, has noticed a bird circling. Not all the students will recognize the significance of the bird for the story, but some will draw on background knowledge to predict that Santiago is interested in this bird because it knows where the small bait fish are swimming. They can then infer that the marlin Santiago seeks would be nearby where the bait fish can be located. The shared reading allows students to draw upon each other's background knowledge then predict that Santiago may soon hook a large fish. Little does Santiago know that he is about to begin an adventure the themes of which resonate for anyone who has sought a meaningful life even in the twenty-first century.

15 Think Alouds and Models

Thinking, and by extension comprehension, is an invisible process. Because we can't see or hear actual thinking, it is a kind of mystery to students how to perform certain cognitive processes. We can observe the products of thinking—an essay, a speech, a response to a question, and so forth—but the processes themselves are locked in the brain and unobservable. Students who struggle with reading tasks may not realize that there is something they can do to grasp what they read with more certainty simply because they have no experience doing so and have never seen, or heard, the processes. Telling students to predict is not enough; teachers must show them how that is done. The think-aloud protocol, often shortened to think-aloud, is one way to make the hidden processes of the brain visible to observers.

In the think-aloud, the reader must be aware of the cognitive processes, like those described in other sections of this book, involved in reading; pause now and then to think about those processes; and be able to discuss the processes (Baumann, Jones, & Seifert-Kessell, 1993). In addition to voicing their thinking, some teachers ask students to write their thoughts in a process similar to the think-aloud (Wilhelm, 2001). When teachers think aloud, they model the thinking processes of competent readers. When teachers model their thinking, students are able to "borrow" the thinking strategies they hear (Cazden, 2001; Wilhelm, 1999). When students think aloud, teachers learn what students are thinking and where their strengths lie. Students may also think aloud in small groups and partner pairs as a means to enhance discussion and model successive approximations of successful cognitive strategies for each other.

STEP BY STEP

1. Teachers can model their own thinking processes by explaining what they notice and wonder about as they read. Read-alouds and shared reading are optimum times for teachers to model for students what good readers are thinking as they read.

2. Students should be encouraged to model their thinking as they read to each other and the teacher. As they do so, they reinforce the cognitive and metacognitive thinking that is required when reading challenging materials. Teachers can learn how to support students who need additional cognitive challenges or who struggle with reading tasks when listening to students thinking aloud.

3. Self-questions coupled with thinking aloud can help students internalize the thinking processes of competent readers. In self-questions, the teacher models thinking about reading by asking questions. Examples are: Does that make sense? Oops, it doesn't. Did it fit? Yes, I'm on the right track (Walker, 2005, p. 689).

APPLICATIONS AND EXAMPLES

Social studies teacher Toni Kinsey wants her students to actively make predictions as they read their textbooks. She uses the think-aloud technique to make her thinking about the reading visible. During a shared reading, her students hear how she makes predictions and asks questions in the context of reading in progress.

IN HER OWN WORDS: Toni Kinsey, South Meadows School, Chelsea, Michigan

This reading section explores the historical and human elements that have shaped present-day Canada. Knowing the origins or the cultural groups and the history of immigration will help prepare students for later debate and persuasive writing topics. I will explain the strategies we will be using all year when we read. This review and modeling will include the goal of reading to construct meaning. Further, after hearing me model the cognitive strategies and practicing them, students will be better equipped to use them on their own and later will become confident in using them each time they read.

While reading the assignment I anticipate that students will have questions. I will model metacognitive processes by reading the first section aloud to the students. I will ask questions, make predictions, and clarify areas that I do not understand. Next, students will begin the reading assignment on their own after I remind them to use the four strategies in order to facilitate their understanding of the reading and to avoid passive reading.

Two questions that I will model in asking about the text include:

Why are there so many European immigrants in Canada while only 5% of all Canadians are people of the First Nations?

How does Canada support the native culture and the different citizen groups?

Both of these topics are addressed in the reading; however, the answer is spread throughout various sections. It will take some thought and time connecting the portions of the reading selection that contain the information. I will show students how to answer the questions by looking at the sections as a whole instead of separate pieces.

In the section of the textbook about European immigrants it is handy to look at the picture of the French and Indian War and see the suffering of the British. Without reading the selection, students may predict that the French and people of the First Nations won the battle. Another prediction I will model is that the areas where most Canadians live are in the southern regions. By looking at the map of geographic features my students and I will be able to predict the settlement areas prior to reading the section entitled, "Where do most Canadians live?" I will predict aloud that the rugged terrain and cold climate in the North makes the newest territory, gained in 1999 by the Inuit, Nunavut, less habitable. Each of these predictions will become important to discussions later in the unit.

16 Question Answer Relationships (QAR)

Many teachers have asked students to respond to a question only to have them parrot or copy a response that contains key words from the question but that, nevertheless, does not actually answer the question or demonstrate any intellectual engagement with the task. This student behavior should not be characterized as laziness or viewed as a reflection of the students' intelligence. On the contrary, it is caused by a lack of training students to attend to the sources of information available to them in making sense of the materials they read (or to which they listen or view). A classroom structure designed to assist the reader to understand what sources of information they may call upon in responding to or creating questions is called the Question Answer Relationship (QAR) (Raphael, 1984).

Training in QARs helps students to establish what they have been asked and then how to identify a response that is appropriate to the type of question. The QAR structure is designed around the premise that questions are not asked in isolation from each other or the text. For example, a question asking about the implications of President Truman's decision to drop a nuclear weapon on Japan during World War II might be a scriptally implicit question calling for students to employ prior knowledge after reading one passage, but it might require a response to information literally contained in the passage of a different text. There are four types of QARs (Raphael, 1986); in the first two question types, students rely on information directly in the text. In the third and fourth question types, students relate what they know from background or prior knowledge with what they read in the text:

1. Questions that call for students to identify what is literally in the text are "Right there." These are usually found in one or two sentences within the passage to which a question refers.

2. Questions that call for students to make textually implicit assumptions or inferences in order to determine an appropriate response from two or more parts of the text are textually implicit and termed "Figure it out" or "Think and search."

3. Questions that call for students to draw upon their background or prior knowledge and join that with what they have read are known as "Author and me" questions. The key differentiation, according to Raphael, is that to understand the question itself, one must have read the text. In section 8 of part II, we referred to a story by Hemingway (1952); if we had asked why Schatz thought he was going to die, the question only makes sense if you had read enough of the story to understand who Schatz is and his condition during the story. Such questions call for a scriptally implicit inference to be made.

4. Questions that call for students to use the information from the story in order to apply it or evaluate the information are similarly required to draw upon background or prior knowledge. Students who are asked what they might feel if they were Schatz in the Hemingway story will not respond correctly unless they consider the characteristics of Schatz as they have learned them from reading the story. This distinction often eludes students and confounds teachers who may think that, because they were asked what they themselves would do, any response is acceptable. These questions we call "On my own."

Note that question types 2 and 3 call for students to make inferences of two different types (cognitive strategy 8). In question type 2, students make connections among parts of the same text. However, in question type 3, students must draw on background and prior knowledge (which can include other texts with which students are familiar) as information sources to construct a response. As we noted in cognitive strategy 9, questions are helpful tools for teachers and students alike in looking ahead to what a text might reveal and focusing attention on relevant aspects of a text in order to make good predictions.

STEP BY STEP

1. Use short passages to demonstrate the types of questions and how responses may be located using different sources of information: a specific location within a text, multiple locations within a text, integrating information that is text dependent, and evaluating or applying that information.

2. As students are learning to think about the types of questions they have been asked, it is helpful for the teacher to provide a line or space under the question (Raphael, 1984). This provides a scaffold for them to think about what type of question has been asked and a reminder about how to locate that information. As an example, refer to the story "August Heat" in section 17.

3. In "August Heat," the stone mason is putting the finishing touches on a monument for an exhibition. How might the marble used in this monument convey a sense of what is to come later in the story?

   Right there: _____

   Figure it out: _____

   Author and me: _____

   On my own: _____

4. Permit students to use the QAR structure as a discussion tool rather than require all their responses in writing, which slows down the processing of what has been read. Help students, through discussion, to respond not only with the answers to questions, but to consider how they used different sources of information and knowledge of types of questions to craft a response.

APPLICATIONS AND EXAMPLES

Secondary Classroom. In cognitive strategy 8, you read about Dryer Thackston's twelfth-grade students using questions to help them understand an essay before, during, and after reading. Mr. Thackston has provided a copy of the essay to students on which they can highlight important concepts and annotate their thoughts. Below, note how Mr. Thackston uses the QAR on the same reading passage to assist students in reading a difficult text and being able to think about that text on multiple levels.

IN HIS OWN WORDS: Using a QAR to Understand That a Conk Is More Than Style

What does a hair style tell about a person? For Malcolm X, it can reveal a great deal about a person's morality. My own grade-level English 12 students complete a unit called Voices of Others that has as its theme how people feel about living on the margins of society. As a part of this unit, students read "Hair" (Malcolm X, 1997), an excerpt from Malcolm X's autobiography, in which he discusses how his judgment of beauty had become so aligned to white standards that he endured a painful chemical treatment to straighten his hair. The learning objectives are for students to read the passage and understand Malcolm X's point and then relate it to their experiences or observations. The passage is only 819 words long and has a 6.0 Flesch-Kincaid readability grade-level rating. Despite the shortness of the passage and the relative ease of the reading, many of my students do not understand Malcolm X's main point, which is that by trying to live up to someone else's standards he had degraded himself.

Students will have difficulty relating to some of the colloquial terms and phrases used in the passage, such as school me, congolene, and conk, as well as the concept of conking one's hair. Many students do not know what lye is so they will not recognize Red Devil as a brand of lye. On a more abstract level, they may have difficulty understanding how straightening one's hair is a form of self-degradation. I will front load most of these vocabulary items before we begin reading, and I will guide students to the more abstract meaning through the use of guiding questions (Davis, 2004).

I have decided to use a Question Answer Relationship (QAR) (Raphael, 1984, 1986) activity (Figure 16.1) to help my students better comprehend the excerpt. Asking students questions before reading helps them to focus on important aspects of the reading (Alvermann & Phelps, 2005; Chapman & King, 2003). QARs serve this purpose as well as explicitly guiding the student's responses to the types of questions being asked and to the reading itself. Effective readers use prior knowledge to better comprehend their reading (Davis, 2004) and the QAR teaches this purposefully. Another advantage is that the questions promote specific types of thinking in students; in this case the figure it out questions require students to draw inferences from the text, which is difficult for many students. Using QARs will help my students better comprehend the Malcolm X excerpt and make them aware of different reading and learning strategies that they can use to better comprehend other readings. QARs help students master content and develop skills that they can continue to use long after they may have forgotten about Malcolm X and his conk.

Many of my struggling-on-grade-level English 12 students do not think about their relationship to the reading or the questions being asked. This strategy will help these students because it states those relationships outright (Raphael, 1984). By knowing where the information is located, students know whether returning to the text will be a useful strategy for answering a question or whether it would be better to examine their own prior knowledge and experience. Many of these students also have a difficult time discerning important facts from unimportant facts, but knowing the

Figure 16.1   QAR Reading Guide: Malcolm X's First Conk

Directions: Read the questions below and then read the excerpt from *The Autobiography of Malcolm X* (1997). On your own paper, answer each question in complete sentences. Where appropriate, give specific examples to support your answers and help you explain them.

Right there: In addition to writing your answer to the following questions, mark and label the part of the excerpt that will answer the following questions:

1. How much money does Malcolm X say he will save when Shorty "[schools]" or teaches him how to give himself a conk?
2. Why did Shorty have Malcolm X feel the outside of the jar of congolene before he put it on Malcolm's hair?
3. What is the belief that Malcolm X says many "Negro men and women in America who are brainwashed into believing"?

Figure it out: The answers to the following questions are stated directly. You will have to answer them by inferring the answers. Mark and label the passages that lead to your answers to these questions:

1. How substantial is the amount of money that Malcolm X saves by having Shorty conk his hair? (Don't focus on the dollar amount. Look for something in the story to compare with the barber's price for a conk.)
2. Why does Malcolm X curse at Shorty while his hair is being rinsed?
3. According to Malcolm X, what are the moral implications of conking one's hair?

Author and me: You will have to use clues from the text as well as your own knowledge to answer these questions:

1. What purpose do the Vaseline, rubber apron, and gloves serve since they are not ingredients?
2. Why would African Americans at the time want to look "white"?
3. Why would Malcolm X call such African Americans "brainwashed"?

On my own: Answer the following questions by using your own experiences and observations:

1. Where do standards of beauty come from today?
2. What do people do to their bodies today that Malcolm X might find objectionable?
3. Are hairstyles or any of your answers to the previous questions moral decisions? Why or why not?

questions in advance will help focus on the more important facts (Alvermann & Phelps, 2005; Chapman & King, 2003).

The QAR can help students understand how Malcolm X felt marginalized in a society that defined beauty in terms that he, as an African American, could not possibly meet. Many of my students feel marginalized in school because they cannot comprehend the same texts some of their classmates readily comprehend. By giving students the QAR, they can comprehend X's message and develop reading and thinking skills that may lead them to feeling less marginalized.

17 The Directed Reading–Thinking Activity

When you read the title of this section, what did you think you would find out by reading? Perhaps you thought that the directed reading–thinking activity had something to do with thinking; then perhaps you thought that was too obvious. Nope, good prediction; keep reading to see what you find out. Maybe you predicted that this is the newest strategy from some university researcher with an acronym to match. This is also a good prediction; keep reading to find out. Now that you've read this paragraph, you might think this section will give you some ideas about how to connect cognitive processes and texts.

The directed reading–thinking activity, DR–TA, as Stauffer explained it (1969), differed from the before reading–during reading–after reading planning sequence that has been the staple of reading teachers since Emmett Betts (1946) described the directed reading activity in the middle of the last century. Betts proposed that teachers should take an active role in developing readiness for reading (often called prereading), guiding the purposes for reading, and so on. Stauffer suggested, instead, that readers could learn to set their own purposes for reading, identify appropriate cognitive strategies to approach the text, make aesthetic connections with text, generalize from principles in the text to other texts and situations, and so on. The teacher's role in the DR–TA is to provide structures and guidance that promote student independence. While Stauffer highlighted the differences between his DR–TA and Betts' directed reading activity, we don't view the two roles as incompatible. Teachers can prepare and guide students and promote students' independent use of cognitive strategies at the same time. The authors of the Cognitive Academic Language Learning Approach (Chamot & O'Malley, 1994) suggest that teachers gradually release responsibility for implementation of cognitive strategies over time until students are able to use and evaluate a given strategy independently. Often, the DR–TA is integrated in context of the before–during–after structure (e.g., Fisher, Brozo, Frey, & Ivey, 2007).

The DR–TA is a classroom structure teachers can use to promote independent use of the prediction strategy. DR–TA, like many of the classroom structures described in this book, is highly adaptable; it can be used in a variety of ways. DR–TAs work well in small groups, with individuals, and in whole class settings. Students may write their predictions, the teacher may do so, or the predictions may simply promote discussion without formal structures like worksheets or reader-response journals.

STEP BY STEP

1. The teacher determines stopping points in the text where prediction and discussion of the predictions might logically occur. Many teachers provide a large index card or blank piece of paper to cover remaining text beyond the stopping point on the page. In this way, students are encouraged to stop and think about their reading rather than simply plowing ahead while other students catch up. Students learn to evaluate and determine their own purposes for reading.

2. For texts with illustrations, maps, and charts, ask students to preview the chapter or section looking specifically at these features and others like words in bold type and end materials for the chapter to gain some idea of the topics for the chapter. In other texts, typically fiction, ask students to read the title. Once students have done this, the teacher asks, "What do you think the story (or chapter) will be about?" Students volunteer predictions. These may be

recorded on the chalkboard, on chart paper, or in the students' reader-response journals. Teachers often note the predictions mentally without recording them in writing to facilitate the discussion. Students can be prompted to elaborate on their predictions with a question such as, "Why do you think that?"

3. Students then read silently or in shared reading to the first stopping point.

4. Teachers may then ask students to summarize by asking, "What have we learned, so far, in the reading?" At this point in the reading, it is worthwhile to review the predictions from the last stopping point to determine if the predictions are still possible or if they should be discarded. New predictions should be volunteered and reasons for the predictions, based on the reading, should be sought. Vacca and Vacca (2005) suggest that explicitly attributing a prediction that has been refuted may not produce a desirable result. We suggest that teachers consider the tone and manner in which predictions are evaluated as reading progresses without attributing the prediction to a specific student.

5. Continue reading to stopping points while engaging in the prediction–validation–refutation cycle until the end of the section or story.

APPLICATIONS AND EXAMPLES

The DR–TA is an adaptable structure; if students are viewing a video or film instead of reading, a directed reading–viewing procedure might be in order (Cunningham, Cunningham, & Arthur, 1981). If students are listening to a guest speaker, the "R" for reading might be substituted for an "L" as in listening, helping students think about what they are learning regardless of the media or text type.

As you read this section, did you notice that you made predictions based on background and prior knowledge, then adjusted those predictions as you gained additional information by reading? The DR–TA is a tool teachers use to assist students in becoming autonomous readers who can engage in predictive tasks just as you did in your reading. In the following text, we provide an example of a DR–TA used with a small group in a discussion format. As students move through the story, they also create a need to know what happens next; motivation for reading becomes an intrinsic part of the readers' repertoires. In this example, note that the reader doesn't impose preconceived constructions about the content on the students. If the teacher doesn't maintain neutrality about each prediction, the students will quickly come to rely on the teacher's construction of the text's meaning rather than learn to do so on their own (Johnston, 1993).

"AUGUST HEAT" BY W. F. HARVEY (1910)

Teacher: Now what could a story titled "August Heat" be about?

Student 1: Well, it is probably about something that happened one very hot summer.

Student 2: Yes, but it might be a story about a police officer.

Teacher: The police? Why do you. . .

Student 2: Sometimes the police were called "the heat" in the past.

Teacher: Okay, anything else? Other ideas? Then open your book and read to the bottom of page one.

Phenistone Road, Clapham,

August 20th, 190—.

I have had what I believe to be the most remarkable day in my life, and while the events are still fresh in my mind, I wish to put them down on paper as clearly as possible.

Let me say at the outset that my name is James Clarence Withencroft.

I am forty years old, in perfect health, never having known a day's illness.

By profession I am an artist, not a very successful one, but I earn enough money by my black-and-white work to satisfy my necessary wants.

My only near relative, a sister, died five years ago, so that I am independent. I breakfasted this morning at nine, and after glancing through the morning paper I lighted my pipe and proceeded to let my mind wander in the hope that I might chance upon some subject for my pencil.

The room, though door and windows were open, was oppressively hot, and I had just made up my mind that the coolest and most comfortable place in the neighbourhood would be the deep end of the public swimming bath, when the idea came.

I began to draw. So intent was I on my work that I left my lunch untouched, only stopping work when the clock of St. Jude's struck four.

The final result, for a hurried sketch, was, I felt sure, the best thing I had done. It showed a criminal in the dock immediately after the judge had pronounced sentence. The man was fat—enormously fat. The flesh hung in rolls about his chin; it creased his huge, stumpy neck. He was clean shaven (perhaps I should say a few days before he must have been clean shaven) and almost bald. He stood in the dock, his short, clumsy fingers clasping the rail, looking straight in front of him. The feeling that his expression conveyed was not so much one of horror as of utter, absolute collapse.

There seemed nothing in the man strong enough to sustain that mountain of flesh.

I rolled up the sketch, and without quite knowing why, placed it in my pocket. Then with the rare sense of happiness which the knowledge of a good thing well done gives, I left the house.

Teacher: Okay. Now, what do you think?

Student 2: Well, there's an artist who works at home. And he's drawn a picture of a criminal standing at the dock. I'm not sure what that means.

Student 3: Me, neither. "Dock" doesn't sound like a place to tie up a boat the way it's used in this story. It sounds like part of a courtroom. Anyway, we were right about one thing. The story is set in summer when it's hot.

Teacher: Right. What did you read that confirmed this prediction?

Student 3: Well, it says right here in the sixth paragraph that it was "oppressively hot."

Teacher: Ah. Right. The artist is about to go somewhere. What do you think?

Student 4: He's going to go swimming? I think the public bath is a swimming pool.

Teacher: Could be. What else?

Student 1: He's a relative of the man in the courtroom. He's going to go visit him in jail, maybe.

Teacher: Okay, read to the middle of the next page; put your index card just under the word *death*.

I believe that I set out with the idea of calling upon Trenton, for I remember walking along Lytton Street and turning to the right along Gilchrist Road at the bottom of the hill where the men were at work on the new tram lines.

From there onwards I have only the vaguest recollection of where I went. The one thing of which I was fully conscious was the awful heat, that came up from the dusty asphalt pavement as an almost palpable wave. I longed for the thunder promised by the great banks of copper-coloured cloud that hung low over the western sky.

I must have walked five or six miles, when a small boy roused me from my reverie by asking the time.

It was twenty minutes to seven.

When he left me I began to take stock of my bearings. I found myself standing before a gate that led into a yard bordered by a strip of thirsty earth, where there were flowers, purple stock and scarlet geranium. Above the entrance was a board with the inscription—

Chs. Atkinson. Monumental Mason.
Worker in English and Italian Marbles

From the yard itself came a cheery whistle, the noise of hammer blows, and the cold sound of steel meeting stone.

A sudden impulse made me enter.

A man was sitting with his back towards me, busy at work on a slab of curiously veined marble. He turned round as he heard my steps and I stopped short.

It was the man I had been drawing, whose portrait lay in my pocket.

He sat there, huge and elephantine, the sweat pouring from his scalp, which he wiped with a red silk handkerchief. But though the face was the same, the expression was absolutely different.

He greeted me smiling, as if we were old friends, and shook my hand.

I apologised for my intrusion.

"Everything is hot and glary outside," I said. "This seems an oasis in the wilderness."

"I don't know about the oasis," he replied, "but it certainly is hot, as hot as hell. Take a seat, sir!"

He pointed to the end of the gravestone on which he was at work, and I sat down.

"That's a beautiful piece of stone you've got hold of," I said.

He shook his head. "In a way it is," he answered; "the surface here is as fine as anything you could wish, but there's a big flaw at the back, though I don't expect you'd ever notice it. I could never make really a good job of a bit of marble like that. It would be all right in the summer like this; it wouldn't mind the blasted heat. But wait till the winter comes. There's nothing quite like frost to find out the weak points in stone."

"Then what's it for?" I asked.

The man burst out laughing.

"You'd hardly believe me if I was to tell you it's for an exhibition, but it's the truth. Artists have exhibitions: so do grocers and butchers; we have them too. All the latest little things in headstones, you know."

He went on to talk of marbles, which sort best withstood wind and rain, and which were easiest to work; then of his garden and a new sort of carnation he had bought. At the end of every other minute he would drop his tools, wipe his shining head, and curse the heat.

I said little, for I felt uneasy. There was something unnatural, uncanny, in meeting this man.

I tried at first to persuade myself that I had seen him before, that his face, unknown to me, had found a place in some out-of-the-way corner of my memory, but I knew that I was practising little more than a plausible piece of self-deception.

Mr. Atkinson finished his work, spat on the ground, and got up with a sigh of relief.

"There! What do you think of that?" he said, with an air of evident pride. The inscription which I read for the first time was this—

Sacred To The Memory Of

James Clarence Withencroft. Born Jan. 18th, 1860.
He Passed Away Very Suddenly
On August 20th, 190—
"In the midst of life we are in death."

Some students flip back the pages of the story to check the name of the narrator. Then the teacher asks a question.

Teacher: That's interesting. Now what do you think?

Student 5: OK—these two guys know each other and the stone mason is playing a practical joke.

Student 1: Hmmm. Maybe, but they don't seem to know each other once Withencroft enters the stone mason's shop. Maybe it's some sort of time shift where one or the other went forward in time.

Teacher: You may be right. What else?

Student 2: Well, the two guys don't seem to know each other, but Atkinson has created a gravestone with Withencroft's name on it. We might find out how that happened on the next page.

Teacher: Let's find out. Read the next section to the words, ". . . but I knew what he meant."

For some time I sat in silence. Then a cold shudder ran down my spine. I asked him where he had seen the name.

"Oh, I didn't see it anywhere," replied Mr. Atkinson. "I wanted some name, and I put down the first that came into my head. Why do you want to know?"

"It's a strange coincidence, but it happens to be mine." He gave a long, low whistle.

"And the dates?"

"I can only answer for one of them, and that's correct."

"It's a rum go!" he said.

But he knew less than I did. I told him of my morning's work. I took the sketch from my pocket and showed it to him. As he looked, the expression of his face altered until it became more and more like that of the man I had drawn.

"And it was only the day before yesterday," he said, "that I told Maria there were no such things as ghosts!"

Neither of us had seen a ghost, but I knew what he meant.

Student 2: [summarizing] Wow, Atkinson carves a gravestone with Withencroft's name on it and Withencroft has drawn a picture of someone who looks like Atkinson in a courtroom. Okay, it looks like something is going to happen. I think we'll find out how these two guys know each other.

Student 4: Yeah, the two must know each other and just don't remember. Maybe this is one of those mysteries where one guy cheated the other one in a card game.

Teacher: All right. Anything else? What about the stone with the crack in it?

Student 5: Oh, right. Maybe the stone is going to fall on Withencroft.

Teacher: Perhaps. Let's read to the end of the next page to see how things turn out.

"You probably heard my name," I said.

"And you must have seen me somewhere and have forgotten it! Were you at Clacton-on-Sea last July?"

I had never been to Clacton in my life. We were silent for some time. We were both looking at the same thing, the two dates on the gravestone, and one was right.

"Come inside and have some supper," said Mr. Atkinson.

His wife was a cheerful little woman, with the flaky red cheeks of the country-bred. Her husband introduced me as a friend of his who was an artist. The result was unfortunate, for after the sardines and watercress had been removed, she brought out a Doré Bible, and I had to sit and express my admiration for nearly half an hour.

I went outside, and found Atkinson sitting on the gravestone smoking.

We resumed the conversation at the point we had left off. "You must excuse my asking," I said, "but do you know of anything you've done for which you could be put on trial?"

He shook his head. "I'm not a bankrupt, the business is prosperous enough. Three years ago I gave turkeys to some of the guardians at Christmas, but that's all I can think of. And they were small ones, too," he added as an afterthought.

He got up, fetched a can from the porch, and began to water the flowers. "Twice a day regular in the hot weather," he said, "and then the heat sometimes gets the better of the delicate ones.

And ferns, good Lord! they could never stand it. Where do you live?"

I told him my address. It would take an hour's quick walk to get back home.

"It's like this," he said. "Well, look at the matter straight. If you go back home to-night, you take your chance of accidents. A cart may run over you, and there's always banana skins and orange peel, to say nothing of fallen ladders."

He spoke of the improbable with an intense seriousness that would have been laughable six hours before. But I did not laugh.

"The best thing we can do," he continued, "is for you to stay here till twelve o'clock. We'll go upstairs and smoke, it may be cooler inside."

To my surprise I agreed.

Student 3: I know. The stone guy is going to knock off Withencroft.

Student 4: Maybe, but the Atkinson doesn't seem to have a reason to kill him. I think there will be an accident and Atkinson will be blamed for it.

The discussion continues, then the teacher summarizes the predictions the group has identified.

> *Teacher:* Okay, we predict that there will be an accident where Atkinson is blamed, that there will be an accident and Atkinson will testify in court about it, or that there will be a twist in the plot and Withencroft finally is overcome by the heat and kills Atkinson. Please read to the end of the story to find out.

We are sitting now in a long, low room beneath the eaves. Atkinson has sent his wife to bed. He himself is busy sharpening some tools at a little oilstone, smoking one of my cigars the while.

The air seems charged with thunder. I am writing this at a shaky table before the open window.

The leg is cracked, and Atkinson, who seems a handy man with his tools, is going to mend it as soon as he has finished putting an edge on his chisel.

It is after eleven now. I shall be gone in less than an hour.

But the heat is stifling.

It is enough to send a man mad.

> *Teacher:* Well, what do you think happened?
>
> *Student 2:* Is that the end of the story? Where's the last page?
>
> *Teacher:* That's it. The author ended his story at this point to leave the reader wondering how it all turned out. What do you think is an ending that fits the circumstances?

The students discuss possibilities and point out features of the story that lend credence to their predictions. Atkinson is sharpening a chisel and could have killed Withencroft. The table is rickety and Withencroft falls and hurts himself. The conversation continues. In DR–TA, extending and refining comprehension is a key element. The students' discussion demonstrates the increasing accuracy of the predictions as they work through the reading. When done well, the DR–TA helps create an environment that is both conversational (Haggard, 1988) and promotes learning through predictions.

18 Reciprocal Teaching

Paulo Freire (1970) proposed that the roles of teachers and students are not as clearly demarcated as we educators sometimes believe. Freire's book often confounds readers for a variety of reasons; it was written in a time and place and about a segment of the world's population about which teachers in western classrooms today understandably know little. One concept, however, that we think has nearly universal appeal as an educational goal is that of the teacher–student, students–teachers. Simply, teachers have a role as learner in the classroom, and students have (or should have) a role as teacher or leader of their own and others' instruction. Often, Freire's ideal sounds good, but how it works in the increasingly political world of education seems elusive. One classroom structure with potential to help students become the subject or agent for their own learning is reciprocal teaching. In this structure, the teacher models the particular behaviors of good readers; later, students learn to take on the role of teacher to facilitate discussion and model the cognitive strategies of good readers.

In conventional reciprocal teaching, students work in small groups with the teacher who employs a cognitive apprenticeship model (Bruer, 1993; Collins, Brown, & Holum, 1991) with the aim of making the invisible and complex processes of reading visible to the student, a novice reader. Cognitive apprenticeship calls for teachers to employ teaching methods that permit students to learn how expert readers, in this case, think about difficult texts. These methods include the following: (1) The teacher models the expected performance. (2) Students perform a task as the teacher coaches through observation and facilitation throughout the apprenticeship. (3) The teacher makes the task manageable and explicit through scaffolding (Eby, 1998). (4) Students are given the opportunity to verbalize what they have learned and how they process their thinking. (5) The teacher models reflection and provides opportunities for students to do so, comparing their performance with others at the same time. (6) Teachers model and encourage students to pose and solve problems (Freire, 1970) that arise as they think about the content and process of reading a given text. Reciprocal teaching also relies on the idea that learning should be situated in authentic tasks (that is, actual reading of texts rather than isolated instruction in the skills of reading) and that it moves from global conceptualization of the whole task before consideration of the parts.

In approaching difficult reading, students must learn strategies that efficiently direct attention, through self-monitoring, to those aspects of the text most likely to be relevant to the reading task as it is situated in a larger context, say a content-area classroom. In designing reciprocal teaching, Palinscar and Brown (1984) identified four cognitive strategies that their research showed as characterizing the thought processes of good readers. These four cognitive strategies appear in all the adaptations of reciprocal teaching since the researchers first explained their classroom structure in 1984. The four strategies are: summarizing (see part II strategy 11), questioning (see part II strategy 9), clarifying (see part IV), and predicting (the subject of this book). As you have come to realize by now, these four strategies are interrelated, so taking a global approach to instruction relying on reciprocal teaching is of particular value.

Reciprocal teaching, in its original configuration, called for a teacher to work with an individual or small group of students. Many teachers and researchers, sensing the appeal of the structure, have devised a variety of adaptations to make the reciprocal teaching intervention instructionally useful in classrooms with 20 to 40 students in them (e.g., Carter, 1997; Marks et al., 1993). In each variation, the teacher plays a significant role, but students assume increasing responsibility over time for use of the strategies to foster comprehension, monitor comprehension, and advance the group discussion. In the process, the students have an opportunity to see expert modeling from the teacher of the four cognitive strategies, to compare their performance with that of others, and to take on the role of expert reader with scaffolding by the teacher and peers. Engagement with reading tasks is likely to increase for students as they have the opportunity to interact meaningfully as agents (capable of acting independently) in the reading process with the teacher, their peers, and the text (Oldfather, 1995).

STEP BY STEP

1. Determine a format for implementing reciprocal teaching that promotes the concepts of cognitive apprenticeship and student use of the four cognitive strategies: summarizing, questioning, clarifying, and predicting. Marks et al. (1993) observed three possibilities:

   a. Students are divided into large groups of approximately eight students. Within each group, the students are assigned to pair up with one other student. Paired students read the text together, preparing questions, predictions, and clarifications and summaries; the teacher monitors this interaction. After reading, the students return to their large group and a student leader initiates discussion while students address each other, using the initial paired-reading conversation as a scaffold, rather than addressing the teacher.

   b. Students are asked to read the text preparing summaries, questions, clarifications, and predictions, in advance. They then join a large group discussion (a whole class of 7 to 12 students in a special education setting, as reported by Marks et al., 1993) where a leader calls on students to share the products of their cognitive preparation; (e.g., summarization, and so on). The teacher may participate by modeling a question at the inferential level (see part II strategy 8, for examples) and so on. The student leader may not elect to call on the teacher right away. In this adaptation, students progress through the large group discussion by considering one cognitive strategy at a time.

   c. The teacher provides a graphic organizer which characterizes the structure of the text (part II strategy 3). Students read the text independently, noting as they read one prediction, one clarification, one question, and one summary at one point in the text. The teacher provides some instructional mediation in generating questions of various levels of complexity, summarization, and so on. Once students have completed this task, they return to the class but sit in small groups representing learning teams or cooperative learning groups. Using the notes generated that represent the four cognitive strategies, students discuss these within the small group for a predetermined time period. Recalling the coaching nature of reciprocal teaching, the teacher circulates among the groups listening to discussion and interjecting from time to time. When time for small group discussion is over, the students return to the whole-class configuration with the teacher now leading the discussion. Groups may be given time to confer and present their best question for the rest of the class to deliberate. Group presentation of their discussion results, including summaries and reports of prediction and clarification, continues.

2. Ensure that students have ample opportunities to practice the strategies with support from the teacher, in small and large groups with their peers, in response journals, and, of course, any time they are asked to (or choose to) read and study difficult materials.

3. Provide job aids, such as posters and bookmarks, which remind students of these thinking strategies and perhaps provide opportunities for students to include their thoughts in text by writing directly on the text (glossing) or using

sticky notes to do so. Encourage students to share these written products of their thinking with each other and with you, the teacher.

4. Students will not be proficient at all the skills called for in reciprocal teaching, at first. Expect that their performance will improve as they observe models from teachers and peers and monitor their own comprehension over time with multiple texts.

APPLICATIONS AND EXAMPLES

Sara Fratrik uses reciprocal teaching as a classroom structure with the students who receive special education services to help them engage with texts they find challenging.

IN HER OWN WORDS: Sara Fratrik, Aberdeen Middle School, Aberdeen, Maryland

Teachers need to model these processes as they read aloud to show students how to enhance their comprehension. The final step in this process is to allow students to practice using the four skills of predicting, questioning, clarifying, and summarizing on their own. It is important to model the process for a sufficient amount of time and allow many opportunities for student practice for this process to work. I plan to begin modeling reciprocal teaching in my classroom with our social studies unit on early modern Europe. One of the content objectives for this unit is that students will understand the rule of Queen Elizabeth and how it affected England then and now. Our literary objective will be that students will read for information.

The reading assignment I chose to begin with is a one-page excerpt from a section in the book about special people that were relevant to the civilization we are studying. This book series involves age-appropriate pictures and content at a lower reading level. The page includes a picture of the person and a thought-provoking, "author and me" (Raphael, 1986) question at the end of the reading. This book and section of the content and history may be challenging for my students, so reciprocal teaching is a perfect fit for my students, the text, and the learning objectives.

For the first time while introducing reciprocal teaching, I will read the text aloud while my students read along while stopping myself to predict, ask questions, and clarify. The first sentence of the text is a good place to set a prediction. It tells that Queen Elizabeth was only 25 when she became queen. At this point I would ask the students if they thought she would be a good queen or not. I expect that some will say no, because she is too young and will not know what to do, while others will say yes and believe that 25 is old. I will continue reading and revisit this prediction to have students determine if they predicted correctly, predicted incorrectly, or still want to read to see what else they can learn. When you read on a little more, the text tells of the Spanish Armada invading England. The text specifically asks the reader if they will win. This is a great point for a prediction and it is generated by the text. I expect some of my students will use their prior knowledge about what they learned about England and say that it is a big country so the

Spanish will not win, while others will say the Spanish will win because Queen Elizabeth will not know what to do.

During the reading my students will also need some clarification on a few words and concepts. They will probably need to clarify the word armada. The best strategy for this would be to read on for clarification. After the word is introduced the text defines the word. Even if the text did not define the word, reading on would be appropriate because it talks about sailing and warships, thus helping the students to see that the Spanish armada was a group of Spanish warships. Another difficult concept may be the short mention of William Shakespeare in the text. I would recommend that the students research further to better understand the text. The best way would be to use the Internet and read some of Shakespeare's work.

As we read, the students may have some questions. Two questions I predict the students might ask include why the Spanish invaded England and why England set their own ships on fire. The best way to answer these would be with a class discussion during and after reading. These questions involve a lot of "on your own thinking" as they are not pointed out specifically in the text. Finally, students will need to learn to summarize what they have read. Summarization is important because it teaches the students to pick out the important information while putting less effort into the unimportant information. To introduce this part of the strategy I will have a summary (see below) of the text for my students to review and thus have an example to base their future summaries on.

Sample Summary

Queen Elizabeth was a young queen and many people were unsure if she would be a good queen. She proved herself by defeating the Spanish at sea when they invaded England. She was thought to be a good ruler because England became a powerful nation and she took time to be with her subjects.

The key to making reciprocal teaching work is modeling until students can begin to generate questions, predictions, clarifications, and summaries on their own. Once they are able to do this, many opportunities for practice will help the students to do these things whenever they read. This is the whole point to reciprocal teaching.

19 Know–Want to Know–Learn (KWL)

The Know–Want to Know–Learn (KWL) structure (Ogle, 1986) is intuitively appealing, and it is instructionally elegant. It proceeds from the idea that students know something and that what students already know can help them construct new understanding.

New understanding grounded firmly in previous learning is far more likely to stick and become the foundation for further learning. Therefore, KWL potentially scaffolds the complex tasks of associating new understandings with background and prior knowledge and of learning how this association is carried out. The lack of procedural knowledge needed to make inferences about text may interfere with student understanding even when the declarative knowledge—the content—is present.

Strategy selection in any instructional situation is more than just reaching into a grab bag or bag of tricks. In fact, we actively resist the characterization of a bag of tricks. It must be purposeful, and the procedural value of the strategy should be obvious to the student. However, Egan (1999) points out even the best graphic organizer can become repetitive and overly predictable if used too frequently. Fortunately, variations of the KWL exist as a result of inquiry by teachers and teacher educators (see Table 19.1). Each uses prior and background knowledge with a graphic organizer to scaffold procedural knowledge so students develop a habit of thinking that characterizes scholarship: inquiry. The "Want to Know" section of the KWL asks students to predict what they will learn based on the knowledge they already have identified and organized in the "Know" step of the classroom structure.

STEP BY STEP

1. Students work individually, in small groups, or as a whole class (Egan, 1999) to create a graphic organizer (Figure 19.1) divided into three columns. In the first, students identify through brainstorming the existing knowledge they already possess about the instructional topic—What I Know.

2. Once students finish brainstorming, they categorize the types of information students expect to use. Our experience is that this important step is often left out.

3. In the second column, students determine what they want to find out that they don't already know—What I Want to Know.

4. After reading, students complete the third column by putting down what new information they have acquired—What I Learned.

APPLICATIONS AND EXAMPLES

When teacher candidates take classes emphasizing the instructional needs of students learning English in the credential classes we teach, we begin with a KWL chart. Because topics related to bilingual students are often in the newspaper and the talk they hear during their field experiences often emphasize this aspect of education, teacher candidates often have a wide range of knowledge upon which they can draw even before reading the first chapter of the course text. The KWL chart helps them organize this information. Those teacher candidates with misinformation also have an opportunity to reconceptualize their understanding through the process, as well. Then, as students read and participate in other class activities they are able to see how their conceptions of what they want to know change to accommodate the new information. The graphic organizer makes very clear what the teacher candidates have learned and how they have come to this understanding with the result that they are far more likely to remember and use the knowledge.

When Columbus Day approached, kindergarten teacher Chris Iacono wanted to tap what students already knew about this explorer. She wrote about her experience (Figure 19.2).

Table 19.1   Annotated List of KWL Modifications

K-W-C

This adaptation of KWL is designed to assist students to ask questions about problems they encounter in mathematics. In K-W-C (Hyde, 2006), students identify "What do you know for sure?" in the first column; they identify "What are you trying to find out?" in the second column, and then determine, "Are there any special conditions [the C], tricks to watch out for, or things to remember?" in the third column. A space underneath asks students to show how they solve the problem using pictures, numbers, and words.

K-W-E-L

Alatorre-Parks (2001) describes a modification of KWL that helps students focus also on required outcomes by adding the 'E,' "What we are *E*xpected to know."

K-W-L-S

Sippola (1995) emphasizes, by adding a fourth column, those things students *S*till need to learn.

K-N-L

Ridgeway (1999) and Alvermann and Phelps (1998) suggest that students occasionally profess not to want to know anything about the topic. They propose that, in that case, students may *N*eed to know about the topic. Therefore, What I Know—What I Need to Know—What I Learned is the result of this modification.

K-W-L-Q

Schmidt proposes a modification of KWL that specifically promotes and sustains inquiry. K-W-L-Q adds "More Questions" to the graphic organizer "so that students would see that learning is a continuous quest" (1999, p. 789).

K-W-W-L

This modification suggests that students sometimes need to know how to acquire information they need. Bryan (1998) adds a column after "What I Want to Know" titled, "Where I Can Learn This."

K-W-L-A

Students that are able to make connections and assign importance to their learning are more likely to retain information. Mandeville (1994) adds a fourth column to the standard KWL chart: A for Affect. In it, students make personal connections and identify their own, related experiences.

S-T-T-G

Egan (1999) proposes the six-step topical guide with six columns: (A) What I definitely know. (B) What I think I know. (C & D) Read/verify. (E) Questions about the reading. (F) Where to find the answers. This organizer assists students in identifying the depth of their understanding and developing new directions for inquiry.

K-W-L Plus

In this, the first modification, Ogle and Carr (1987) enhanced the original KWL model by asking students to engage in a follow-up activity to reinforce connections and new knowledge and to facilitate transfer of the metacognitive understanding they have acquired in new reading situations. Ogle and Carr suggest mapping information graphically or summarizing.

Figure 19.1   KWL Graphic Organizer

K	W	L
What I Know	**What I Want to Know**	**What I Learned**
Categories		

Figure 19.2a   Ms. Iacono's KWL Chart

Christopher Columbus		
K **what we KNOW**	**W** **what we WANT to know**	**L** **what have we LEARNED**
He's a pirate. Maybe he fixes boats. Catches fish. He drives the boat. He is on a boat in the water. He catches birds.	Is he a pirate? What does he do? Does he help people? Does he help sea turtles? Where is he going in that boat? When is his birthday?	• He is not a pirate. • He is a sailor. • He catches fish. • He goes to new places. • He gave a parrot to the queen. • He traded treasure for food. • He went to an island in America. • His birthday is around September in 1451. • October 12, 1492, is when he landed on the island. • He's dead now.

IN HER OWN WORDS: Christine Iacono, Mary B. Lewis Elementary School, Colton, California

After seeing the blank expressions on my kindergartners' faces when I announced that we were going to learn about Christopher Columbus, I decided to use a modified version of KWL with them. Since none of them truly knew anything about Columbus, I started

Figure 19.2b   Ms. Iacono's KWL Chart

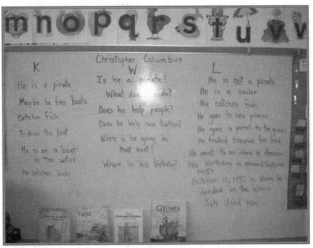

Figure 19.2c   Information Books We Read

Bjorkman, J. (1991). *In 1492*. New York: Scholastic.
Carpenter, E. (1992). *Young Christopher Columbus,*
    discoverer of new worlds. New York: Troll Associates.
Gross, R. B. (1974). *A book about Christopher Columbus.* New
    York Scholastic.
Strong, S. (1991). *The voyage of Columbus in his own words*
    (a pop-up book). Columbia: InterVisual Communications, Inc.

the lesson by displaying several books about Columbus on the bottom tray of the white board. I told students that I was going to read some of the books to them because he was someone famous that I wanted them to know about.

I asked them to look at the covers of the books and think about what they thought the books might tell them about Columbus. I wrote the title of our chart, "Christopher Columbus," and the letters *K, W,* and *L* in different colors on the white board. I explained that we were going to list the things we know about Columbus under the K and the things we want to know under the W before I would read the books. Then, I told them that we would be listing things in the L section after I read to them to find out all the things they learned about Columbus from the books.

The first student answer I wrote in the K section was, "He is a pirate." I asked the student why he thought Columbus was a pirate, and he justified his statement by pointing out the obvious ships on the covers of all the Columbus books. I continued listing their answers and asking them to tell me their reasoning for their answers. We categorized the predictions, orally, as jobs and places where Columbus worked. We moved on to the W section, and the first question was, "Is he a pirate?" The students generated several relative questions; the final question was, "When is his birthday?" Then I chose two of the books and read them aloud to the class. During the reading, whenever I would get to a part of the book that answered their questions from the W section, I could see and hear the "aha" from the group.

After the readings, we started listing the things we learned from the books in the L section of our chart. The first things we listed were, "He is not a pirate," and "He is a sailor." We continued to list the things we learned, but when we looked to see if we had answered all of our questions from the W section, we were missing one answer about Columbus' birthday. Someone thought the book said it was October 12, 1492, but we went back into the book and found that date was not his birthday—it was the day he landed on the island. When I asked them how we could find the answer to our unanswered question, another student came up with "the computer." We logged on to the computer and searched to find a site that gave us some information about his birthday. They were surprised to find out that there was not an exact date listed, and we added the information to our chart even though it wasn't in the book.

The KWL chart was very successful. It made it possible for students to look for relevant clues about Columbus from the covers of the books and justify their ideas. It focused their attention by giving them a purpose during the readings—answering their own questions from the W section, and it helped them organize what they learned from the books. The question about his birthday even extended the lesson to include a technology component that we weren't expecting. We finished with an art project about the three ships in Columbus' fleet.

20 Guided Reading and Summarizing Procedure (GRASP)

In Part II, cognitive strategy 11, we explored how summarization might help students attend to the important attributes of a text and make more precise predictions as a result. Learning to summarize effectively is an important skill, one that a classroom structure with the acronym GRASP (guided reading and summarizing procedure) (Hayes, 1989) can help students to master. Based on summarization rules, this classroom structure is best used as an introduction to the concept of summarizing. Brown, Campione, and Day (1981) suggest the following rules for summarizing:

1. Deleting trivial information. In Figure 20.1a, a student organizes information from a nonfiction article according to what is interesting and what is important.
2. Delete redundant information.
3. Label categories for listed information—army and navy can be recategorized as "military."
4. Identify and relabel subordinate actions to a superordinate—"Sherman marched his army across Tennessee to Atlanta then on to Savannah" can be relabeled as "Sherman marched his army to Savannah."
5. Find and select the author's topic sentence in each paragraph where one exists.
6. Create or invent a topic sentence if the author has not written one into the text.

STEP BY STEP

1. Find a suitable text that ranges from 500 to 1,500 words (Hayes, 1989). Identify the cognitive strategy, summarizing, students will work with and note that they will work in groups for this exercise. Students will also need to know that the procedure they use in groups will also work for them when they have summaries to write as individuals.

2. Students are directed to read the text and remember all they can. After reading, the class lists all they can remember from their reading on a chalkboard or chart paper. At this point, students may be simply retelling all they remember. Students then reread the material to determine if they missed any significant information that should be on their list.

3. Students and teacher review their list to identify the important categories of information represented in the text. The group notes any relationships among the categories they establish.

4. Finally, students write their summary with directions to leave out unimportant information and details, to combine information where they can, and to add information and sentence elements to make the summary coherent. In Figure 20.1b, the student organizes the final summary.

APPLICATIONS AND EXAMPLES

Whitney Johnson uses GRASP with her students when plots become complex. Students using GRASP are able to revisit and reconstruct the plot in their minds as a result of this summarizing activity. Summarization and prediction share a link in that both require attention to relevant details.

IN HER OWN WORDS: Whitney Johnson, Lanier Middle School, Buford, Georgia

In a unit on scary/suspenseful stories, students will read "The Monkey's Paw" (Jacobs, 1902), a short story. After reading the story, students will be able to distinguish between how tone and mood are developed throughout a story, the importance of character motivation in a story, and the sequence of events. In order to help students further understand these concepts, I will use the series-of-events chain, a compare/contrast matrix, and GRASP as study strategies. Using the summaries they create, students will be able to apply their knowledge to the next suspense story in the unit and predict its structure in order to focus more fully on the story.

The GRASP strategy is a thorough way to ensure that students remember certain parts of the story. What I really like about the strategy is that the students write down as much as they can without looking back. I feel that this activates the students' memory and encourages them to not rely on the text. By writing what the students call out on the board as important things to remember as part of the summary, the teacher is also modeling how to delete concepts, regroup them, and identify topics in the summarization process and be more concise. Anything we can use in the classroom to promote thinking with the text is beneficial. Supporting what students read and learn in more than one way will only encourage the important ideas and concepts.

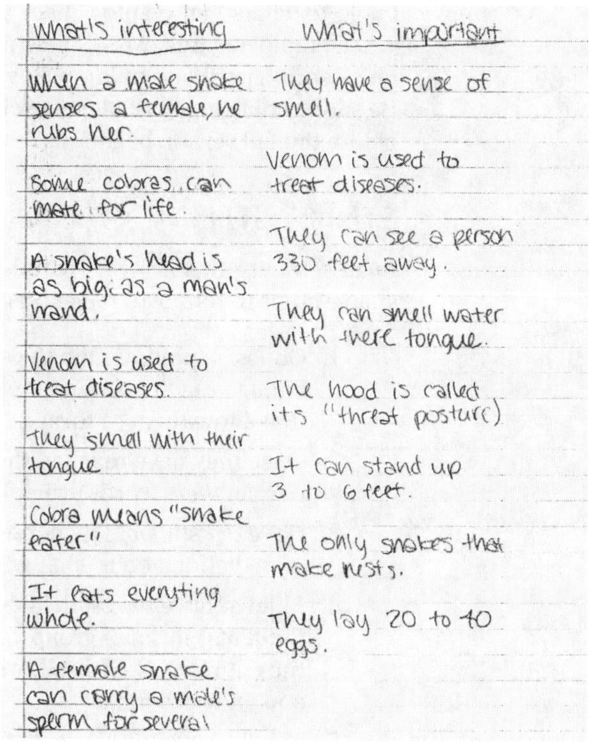

Figure 20.1a   Deleting Trivial Information

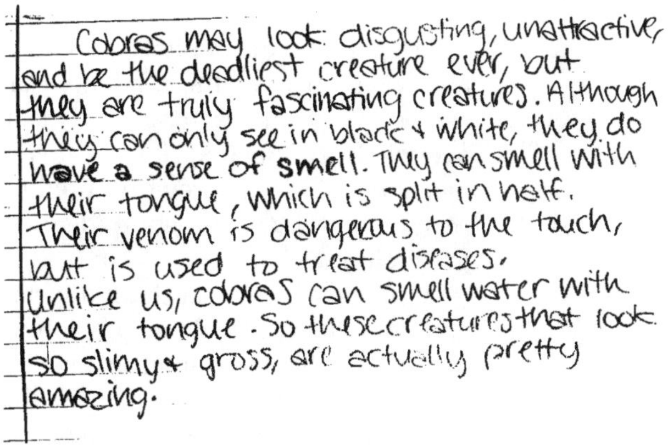

What's interesting	What's important
When a male snake senses a female, he rubs her.	They have a sense of smell.
Some cobras can mate for life.	Venom is used to treat diseases.
A snake's head is as big as a man's hand.	They can see a person 330 feet away.
Venom is used to treat diseases.	They can smell water with there tongue.
They smell with their tongue	The hood is called its "threat posture)
Cobra means "snake eater"	It can stand up 3 to 6 feet.
It eats everyting whole.	The only snakes that make nests.
A female snake can carry a male's sperm for several	They lay 20 to 40 eggs.

Figure 20.1b   GRASP Summary

Cobras may look disgusting, unattractive, and be the deadliest creature ever, but they are truly fascinating creatures. Although they can only see in black & white, they do have a sense of smell. They can smell with their tongue, which is split in half. Their venom is dangerous to the touch, but is used to treat diseases. Unlike us, cobras can smell water with their tongue. So these creatures that look so slimy & gross, are actually pretty amazing.

21   Cliffhanger

The cliffhanger is most often associated with television series when one season ends with some shocking event that leaves the viewer wondering what happened. This plot device begs the viewer (or, in our case, the reader) to predict what is going to happen next. If you are in our generation, you will remember when everyone wanted to know "Who shot JR?" on the TV series *Dallas*. Many authors of extended texts also use this technique. Readers can detect this structure and create a sense of excitement about what might happen next as they read. As with other cognitive strategies described in this book, teachers can employ them to enhance what students mentally do as they read. When employing this classroom structure, note how prediction interacts with other cognitive strategies. Want to know how to implement cliffhangers as a classroom structure? Be sure to tune in next fall. . . . Okay, you win, we will leak the method to you right now before the fall season begins. . . .

STEP BY STEP

In all actuality, this is a very simple reading strategy to implement. There are just a few simple steps to follow to make this tool work.

1. Choose a point within the selected reading to stop, but be sure to include enough reading so that the students have been exposed to evidence and details that allow them to form their predictions.

2. Once they have reached the predetermined stopping point, have them summarize (in *their* words) what has transpired to that point.

3. Have the students gather evidence from the reading that will help them make a prediction about what will happen next (or at the end of the story).

4. I like to have the students share their predictions (and facts supporting their thoughts) in small groups but you could have them share their thoughts with the entire class. This allows for great discussions on different points of view and understanding.

5. Finally, have the students finish the reading (or next section) and then compare their predictions to what actually takes place in the reading (this makes for a great journal entry).

Depending on the length of the reading selection or other source material, you may want to have the students make several predictions at different points. This serves two purposes: first, it breaks up larger material so the students do not become overwhelmed. Second, it provides an opportunity for the students to make adjustments/revisions to previous predictions based on the new information they have read or heard. (It is a good idea to have the students use different colors for each prediction.)

The most important thing you can do as a teacher is to make sure your students feel comfortable with making predictions. You need to reassure them that there is no "wrong" prediction as long as it makes sense given the evidence they provided. It is also very important that teachers make this as enjoyable as possible for the students. Do not make this "just another worksheet" assignment. This is a great way to engage students; do not waste the opportunity.

APPLICATIONS AND EXAMPLES

Chad Semling notes: "This is one of the more effective during-reading strategies I have used. My students not only leave a reading with a greater understanding of the content but also enjoy the process. I have used this strategy with not only reading materials but also classroom lectures and video/multimedia programs. The 'Cliffhanger' not only helps the students develop their perception skills, but it also requires them to evaluate their own understanding and practice summarizing what they have read."

⌒⌒ *IN HIS OWN WORDS:* Chad Semling, Menomonie Middle School, Menomonie, Wisconsin

One example of this strategy in action uses Edgar Allan Poe's "Pit and the Pendulum" as the text. I use this reading as part of a lesson dealing with the Spanish Inquisition. Due to the complex nature of the vocabulary (especially for seventh graders), it is a good idea to pre-teach the terms as much as possible. I also recommend an audio version of the reading or at least reading the selection aloud (shared reading). The following is a sample of the reading that allows the student to gather evidence to make predictions. It should be noted that I usually have the students stop four or five different times throughout this reading due to its length.

"So far I had not opened my eyes. I felt that I lay upon my back unbound. I reached out my hand, and it fell heavily upon something damp and hard. There I suffered it to remain for many minutes, while I strove to imagine where and what I could be. I longed, yet dared not, to employ my vision. I dreaded the first glance at objects around me. It was not that I feared to look upon things horrible, but that I grew aghast lest there should be NOTHING to see. At length, with a wild desperation at heart, I quickly unclosed my eyes. My worst thoughts, then, were confirmed. The blackness of eternal night encompassed me. I struggled for breath. The intensity of the darkness seemed to oppress and stifle me. The atmosphere was intolerably close. I still lay quietly, and made effort to exercise my reason. I brought to mind the inquisitorial proceedings, and attempted from that point to deduce my real condition. The sentence had passed, and it appeared to me that a very long interval of time had since elapsed. Yet not for a moment did I suppose myself actually dead. Such a supposition, notwithstanding what we read in fiction, is altogether inconsistent with real existence;—but where and in what state was I? The condemned to death, I knew, perished usually at the auto-da-fes, and one of these had been held on the very night of the day of my trial. Had I been remanded to my dungeon, to await the next sacrifice, which would not take place for many months? This I at once saw could not be. Victims had been in immediate demand. Moreover my dungeon, as well as all the condemned cells at Toledo, had stone floors, and light was not altogether excluded.

A fearful idea now suddenly drove the blood in torrents upon my heart, and for a brief period I once more relapsed into insensibility. Upon recovering, I at once started to my feet, trembling convulsively in every fiber. I thrust my arms wildly above and around me in all directions. I felt nothing; yet dreaded to move a step, lest I should be impeded by the walls of a TOMB. Perspiration burst from every pore, and stood in cold big beads upon my forehead. The agony of suspense grew at length intolerable, and I cautiously moved forward, with my arms extended, and my eyes straining from their sockets, in the hope of catching some faint ray of light. I proceeded for many paces, but still all was blackness and vacancy. I breathed more freely. It seemed evident that mine was not, at least, the most hideous of fates.

And now, as I still continued to step cautiously onward, there came thronging upon my recollection a thousand vague rumors of the horrors of Toledo. Of the dungeons there had been strange things narrated—fables I had always deemed them—but yet strange, and too ghastly to repeat, save in a whisper. Was I left to perish of starvation in this subterranean world of darkness; or what fate perhaps even more fearful awaited me? That the result would be death, and a death of more than customary bitterness, I knew too well the character of my judges to doubt. The mode and the hour were all that occupied or distracted me.

My outstretched hands at length encountered some solid obstruction. It was a wall, seemingly of stone masonry—very smooth, slimy, and cold. I followed it up; stepping with all the careful distrust with which certain antique narratives had inspired me. This process, however, afforded me no means of ascertaining the dimensions of my dungeon; as I might make its circuit, and return to the point whence I set out, without being aware of the fact, so perfectly uniform seemed the wall. I therefore sought the knife, which had been in my pocket when led into the inquisitorial chamber, but it was gone; my clothes had been exchanged for a wrapper of coarse serge. I had thought of forcing the blade in some minute crevice of the masonry, so as to identify my point of departure. The difficulty, nevertheless, was but trivial, although, in the disorder of my fancy, it seemed at first insuperable. I tore a part of the hem from the robe, and placed the fragment at full length, and at right angles to the wall. In groping my way around the prison, I could not fail to encounter this rag upon completing the circuit. So, at least, I thought, but I had not counted upon the extent of the dungeon, or upon my own weakness. The ground was moist and slippery. I staggered onward for some time, when I stumbled and fell. My excessive fatigue induced me to remain prostrate, and sleep soon overtook me as I lay."

From: http://www.literature.org/authors/poe-edgar-allan/pit-and-pendulum.html

Depending on the material, I either have the students follow a format outlined on an overhead or white-board. However, especially early on, it is a good idea to pass out a sheet with the instructions and guidelines (see Figure 21.1). The "cliff" I use is to help the students visualize the prediction process at each stopping point; feel free to develop your own format.

Figure 21.1   The Cliffhanger

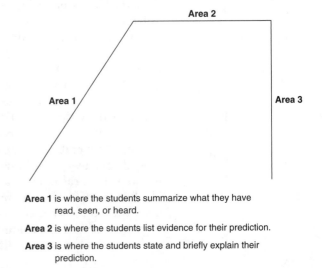

Area 2

Area 1

Area 3

Area 1 is where the students summarize what they have read, seen, or heard.

Area 2 is where the students list evidence for their prediction.

Area 3 is where the students state and briefly explain their prediction.

22 Graphic Organizers

Well-known lesson structures call for teachers to plan what must be done in advance of a lesson that calls for reading (prereading, before reading), what must be done to guide students during reading of challenging texts, and what must be done after the reading in order to focus, remediate, or extend students' understanding of a text passage (e.g., Betts, 1946; Dechant, 1991; Graves & Graves, 1995; Vacca & Vacca, 2005). Graphic organizers fit into the prereading–during reading–after reading model quite well, but as we have asserted in other parts of this book, we encourage teachers to use these tools with precision. A teacher who knows why a specific graphic organizer is appropriate and where it best works in the lesson plan as it relates to the reading students encounter is far more effective in encouraging the cognitive practices students need. The KWL (Ogle, 1986) example in strategy 19 is a good example of a thoughtfully deployed graphic organizer. The organizer helps students think about what they know in advance of reading (or other instructional input) and then predict what they may learn as a result. Just as important, the KWL structure calls for students and the teacher to return to the graphic organizer to make further sense of the material that was completed after reading is done.

However, other graphic organizers may be similarly useful. The well-known Venn diagram is an example. Students might complete a Venn diagram using background and prior knowledge in advance of reading that requires students to compare two different concepts, characters, or sets of information. A comparison matrix may point students in a direction that provides more depth to their thinking. Used in this manner, a graphic organizer may serve to help students make good predictions before or during reading. Similarly, the graphic organizer might assist students to clarify predictions they made earlier during reading or after they have finished a selection from the text.

Using the organization students have imposed on their existing knowledge, students might then read a text passage with the intention of returning to the Venn diagram to reconstruct their knowledge given the new information they have obtained from their reading. As students become proficient at using graphics to impose an organizational pattern on what they learn, teachers should gradually release responsibility for choosing and perhaps creating a suitable graphic organizer to assist in the learning process. Students should know not just that they are required by their teachers to complete a graphic organizer; they should have an explicit understanding of why they use the organizer and why a particular organizer is selected.

STEP BY STEP

1. Choose a suitable graphic organizer that represents the organization pattern of the text students will read. Determine if it will work most efficiently at the prereading, during reading, or after reading phases of a lesson that includes reading material. To encourage prediction, students might be asked to activate existing knowledge (part II strategies 5 and 6) before they begin reading and use the graphic to give order to the material. A blank or partially completed graphic supplied by the teacher may be required to appropriately scaffold the students' experiences. Students might also add to a graphic during reading if the length and complexity of the text suggests this approach.

2. Assist students to determine why you have chosen a specific graphic organizer before or during reading. Doing so after reading may also be appropriate. In

this way, students learn to detect the organizational patterns of the text (see part II strategy 3) through scaffolding questions.

3. As students become increasingly proficient with the use of the graphic organizers, permit them to choose the graphic organizer that seems most appropriate after previewing the material and examining headings, charts, and diagrams (see part II strategy 2). In this way, students learn to predict with increasing accuracy what they will learn and adjust their thinking when new concepts are encountered more frequently.

APPLICATIONS AND EXAMPLES

Sometimes what students believe to be so and what actually is so can create conflict in the mind that must be resolved if learning is to occur. Students might believe that waves indicate that water is in motion, moving toward shore then away from shore. A direct observation seems to confirm this idea. But this rather evident conclusion is not correct. The movement of the water is up and down, roughly perpendicular to the ocean floor underneath. Scientists call this a transverse wave, and readers of this book might picture (visualization in part II strategy 12, remember) two people holding opposite ends of a rope with one person moving it rapidly up and down creating a wave in the string. Notice that the string doesn't move from one person to the other with the wave; instead the waves move up and down. Waves on a beach do much the same thing.

A longitudinal wave, by contrast, moves in parallel to the medium which conducts it. A sound wave is a good example of such a wave. Now, suppose that you have a science text that describes these two wave phenomenon. In addition, you know that your students might believe, by generalization and observation, that the medium (like the water) moves along with the wave. Before the students read the science text that describes these two types of waves, you will need to make several instructional decisions. First, consider students' background knowledge about waves. What about that knowledge will need to change as a result of the learning activities including reading? Second, how is the text organized? Does it describe the transverse wave in one section followed by another section that describes the longitudinal wave? If so, a graphic organizer (Figure 22.1) might be in order that calls students' attention to this structure before they begin reading. Note that students can create this graphic organizer by folding a piece of blank paper into fourths, saving the teacher time standing in front of the copy machine.

✏ *IN HIS OWN WORDS*: A Few Words

Primary grade teachers often employ a technique termed the word sort. Word sorts employ a simple graphic organizer, too. Readers who have used a word sort to assist student learning to read or with spelling patterns recognize the graphic nature of the word sort right away. But, you say, isn't this book about prediction? You're right. Word sorts are powerful tools that help students to make predictions about words. A teacher who wants students to learn about the different correspondences between letters and sounds for the long /e/ might construct a graphic organizer like Figure 22.2. As students work through words pronounced for them or presented on index cards, students must decide where to write the word to match the spelling pattern. When students recognize the spelling pattern they are more able to predict unknown words they encounter in reading and to predict the spelling of words they have not encountered in print before.

Figure 22.1 Waves: An Organizer

Before reading: Draw a picture of a person floating in the waves 15 seconds apart.	
Time index: 0	Time index: 0 minutes 15 seconds
During Reading—Key attributes of transverse waves	During Reading—Key attributes of longitudinal waves
After reading: Draw an illustration (you select the subject) of a transverse wave and another illustration of a longitudinal wave.	
Transverse Wave	Longitudinal Wave

Figure 22. 2 Phoneme–Grapheme Correspondences

e	y	ee	ea	e-e	??
me	very	keep	eat	these	field
be	merry	see	meat	Pete	police
	likely	bee	please	complete	
		beep	treat	create	

Based on Fry, 2004.

23 Anticipation Guides

Children have a lot on their minds; there is so much to learn that the powerful cognitive function of making inferences can be quite helpful, and not just from reading, either. In their early lives, children observe as much as they can from their siblings, parents, playground experiences, teachers, and a multitude of other people and events. From these observations, children make inferences that help them explain and understand the world, develop a framework for dealing with it, and perhaps create theories that give the world and their lives in it purpose and meaning. Inferences, as we've noted in other sections of this book, are characteristic of good thinking habits. Here's a secret: Sometimes our inferences and mental representations (Gardner, 2006) are incorrect or only partially correct. Children, like the adults around them, work from such inferences and representations all the time. What children do with those constructs, and what teachers do to facilitate the process, is the real business of education. Teachers are in the business of changing minds. Gardner suggests that changes of mind may be of two types: deepening one's mental representations and transformation of the existing representations.

Anticipation is the emotion most often associated with prediction. The anticipation guide (Dufflemeyer, Baum, & Merkley, 1987) is a classroom structure with the potential to use prediction as a foundation for confronting the mental representations that exist as background and prior knowledge. Further, the anticipation guide may assist the thinking reader with deepening of existing mental representations or with a transformation of those structures. Once confronted, a thinker can purposefully construct new representations based on the new information presented. An anticipation guide is essentially a set of statements with which a student can agree or disagree or note as likely or unlikely during prereading. Once this existing knowledge is activated, students then read the text with the purpose of accommodating new information that differs from the existing knowledge. Once students realize that they must construct a new mental representation, a during or after reading opportunity should be provided for students to determine the compatibility of their pre-existing knowledge with that presented in the text.

Effective anticipation guides require some preparation and knowledge of students' existing knowledge. The most daunting task for the teacher is in preparation of the statements to which students will respond. Statements used on anticipation guides may be flawed in three important ways (Dufflemeyer, 1994): (1) Students lack sufficient existing knowledge about the topic to form any reasoned judgment—remember we are promoting a change of mind. (2). The statement is based on ideas subordinate to major concepts—remember that new knowledge is constructed in the context of existing knowledge. (3) The statement is common knowledge among students. To that end, effective statements convey major ideas, activate and draw upon students' existing knowledge, are general in nature, and challenge students' current mental representations.

STEP BY STEP

1. Review the text or other instructional material to identify the major concepts represented therein.

2. Construct a series of statements, some supported by the text and others that are not, keeping in mind the principles of statement generation discussed

previously. Include a place for students to check whether they agree or disagree or whether a statement is likely or unlikely to be verified by the text. In most contexts, avoiding true and false options is preferable.

3. Present the statements to students prior to reading. The statements, an anticipation guide, may be presented on a data projector, supplied as a handout, or printed on a chalkboard. Some teachers tally student responses as a means of fostering discussion (Ryder & Graves, 2003); others ask students to compare responses with a partner (Fisher et al., 2007).

4. Students read the text. As they do so, they should attempt to determine if their initial responses are supported by the material or if the material suggests that the response should be changed.

5. After students finish reading, ask them to respond again to the statement using the response option (agree/disagree, likely/unlikely); they should also be asked to explain why their initial responses were or were not supported, encouraging them to confront the compatibility of pre-existing mental representations with what is in the text. This is often done in writing as part of an extended anticipation guide (Dufflemeyer & Baum, 1992). Teachers may choose to re-tally student responses to foster discussion among class members or ask students to compare revised responses with a partner or in a small group, again supporting the revised opinion based on the reading. We suggest that students may benefit if encouraged to find additional sources to support or push back against the text under consideration.

APPLICATIONS AND EXAMPLES

Mrs. Trish Schafer uses the anticipation guide to deepen students' knowledge and challenge beliefs that might otherwise hinder learning about ancient river civilizations. Notice that she returns to the anticipation guide after reading and provides students with an opportunity to use the text to support their new understanding.

IN HER OWN WORDS: Tricia Sents Schafer, Camden High School, Camden, New York

The textbook is broken into four sections; each section teaches students about a different ancient empire. Throughout our study of early civilizations we focus on how geography influenced the development of each unique civilization, and how later empires borrowed ideas from earlier empires. Thus far, my ninth-grade class has studied the Sumerian Civilization of Mesopotamia. As we begin our study of ancient Egypt, I will consistently refer back to ancient Sumer, so students can compare and contrast the technology, belief systems, inventions, government, and geography of these two civilizations. In order to prepare my students to read about the effects the Nile River had on Egyptian civilization, I created an anticipation guide. The guide includes five statements based on the reading assignment. My ninth-grade students will read each statement, and agree or disagree with each statement. In addition, students will be asked to justify their responses with a simple explanation as to whether they agreed or disagreed (Figure 23.1).

Figure 23.1   Anticipation Guide

Before Reading			After Reading	
Agree	Disagree		Agree	Disagree
_____	_____	1. Floods are always destructive.	_____	_____
_____	_____	2. Growing food in a desert is impossible.	_____	_____
_____	_____	3. Floods are unpredictable.	_____	_____
_____	_____	4. The Nile River was worshipped as a god.	_____	_____
_____	_____	5. It is unwise to build settlements near rivers.	_____	_____

After completing the anticipation guide, students will share their answers to the questions in their small groups and discuss why they agreed or disagreed with the statements. Based on our previous study of ancient Sumer students might recall that floods are not always destructive. In fact, yearly flooding allowed the Sumerians to farm in the middle of the desert. The floods would wash rich deposits of black silt onto the river banks, and the Sumerians used this soil to fertilize their fields. Thus it follows students may generalize that a certain amount of flooding is necessary in order to be able to farm in the desert. In Sumer, the Tigris and Euphrates Rivers were unpredictable; therefore, dikes were built to prevent villages from being flooded. Students may believe this is always true of floods. However, as students read the paragraphs I will assign, they will discover that in ancient Egypt the flooding of the Nile was quite predictable and allowed them to establish a yearly cycle of flood, plant, harvest.

Students will be asked to read a section of the text about ancient Egypt. After reading the section, students will revisit their anticipation guide and change any of their answers that may have been wrong. Students will return to their small groups for discussion and to support their changed responses.

24 Metacognitive Double-Entry Journals

Journals and note-taking strategies help students organize their thoughts, provide a reference for later study, and afford an opportunity to think about a concept on the reader's (or thinker's) own terms. However, teachers notice that the journals students write sometimes lack substance or higher levels of cognitive activity. In part II strategy 3 we explored a double-entry journal that directs students' attention toward the features of the text. Here, you'll learn about a metacognitive double-entry journal which provides a form of support that helps students realize that different types of cognitive activity occur during reading (Burns, 2004). As students write their double-entry journals, they follow a traditional procedure of placing their direct observations from the story in one column (note-taking) and their comments on the opposite side (note-making) (see Figure 24.1).

However, after extensive modeling, students also learn to code their journals in the left-hand margin with a number which corresponds to one of six strategies (see Table 24.1). You will see that strategy number four asks students to make focal predictions about word meanings, strategy 2 asks students to make global predictions about events in the text and how they relate to each other, strategy 5 asks students to make inferences, and strategy 3 asks students to think about questions that can lead to predictions and clarifications as they read.

STEP BY STEP

1. Select an appropriate text passage and use a think-aloud protocol to model for students how each strategy is identified as you read, how to take notes in the left-hand column, and how to make notes in the right-hand column. Then model how to code the strategy in the margin. Each note-taking entry in the double-entry journal also includes the page number and sentence from the text that prompted the student to write the entry.

2. Have students try this on their own. Small group work may make this technique manageable for students who struggle with the concept of identifying the strategy; (e.g., guessing a word meaning, predicting what happens next, etc.).

APPLICATIONS AND EXAMPLES

When Dr. Burns first implemented the metacognitive double-entry journal with her fourth-grade students, she found that they often struggled with the process of slowing down the reading process to record their thoughts in the journal. Students also recorded shorter sentences instead of working with the ideas in longer sentences because they did not want to write down the longer sentences. As a result, she modified her strategy to allow students to simply record the page number where the passage that prompted the metacognitive realization appeared. In order to make the tool comprehensible for her students, she also changed the term *note-taking* to *What the story says* and the term *note-making* to *What I think*. Tiffany, a third-grade student in Dr. Burns' class, created a double-entry metacognitive journal for *Balto, The Dog Who Saved Nome* (Davidson, 1996) (Figures 24.1a and 24.1b).

Table 24.1   Comprehension Strategies for Metacognitive Thinking

1. Create pictures in your mind about the text.
2. Predict what will happen next.
3. Ask yourself questions about the text.
4. Personalize the text based on your own experiences.
5. Guess the meanings of words during reading.
6. Go back and reread when the text doesn't make sense.

Figure 24.1a Tiffany's Metacognitive Double-Entry Journal

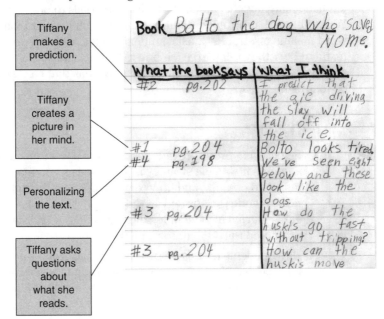

Tiffany makes a prediction.

Tiffany creates a picture in her mind.

Personalizing the text.

Tiffany asks questions about what she reads.

Book _Balto the dog who saved Nome._

What the book says		What I think
#2	pg.202	I predict that the aic driving the slay will fall off into the ice.
#1	pg.204	Bolto looks tired
#4	pg.198	We've seen eight below and these look like the dogs.
#3	pg.204	How do the huskls go fast without tripping?
#3	pg.204	How can the huski's move

Figure 24.1b Josh's Metacognitive Double–Entry Journal

Double-Entry Journals

Book _Sarah, Plain and tall_ great Josh ✓+

What the story says	What I think
4 Pg. 16	When Erika got up early in the morning to pick up her Grandmother like Papa it the kids got up early to pick up Sarah
4 Pg. 16	When Hayden went to go out and gave water to a horse its relating when Papa gave water to a horse
2 Pg. 18	I predict that Sarahs cat will like the house better than the one at the sea. ✓
3 Pg. 20	I wonder why Sarah was so worried about this? – more specific
1 Pg. 20	When Sarah gave the stone to Annah I imagined it was sparkli and white and pretty

25 Hot Seat

The hot seat is a cooperative learning strategy that fosters learning from predictions. In hot seat, students adopt the persona of a character in literature or history then answer questions from the character's perspective.

STEP BY STEP: HOT SEAT

1. Divide the class into groups of three to five students.
2. Each student selects or is assigned a character whose persona he or she will adopt.
3. Group members create questions based on their understanding of the story or text to be asked of the other characters in the group.
4. Then, in turn, each character responds to questions posed by other members of the group. A two-minute time limit is suggested.
5. As a clarification strategy, students might write down their predictions and points of confusion and use these as a basis for the questions they have for other members of the group. By focusing their questions toward specific characters represented by group members, students also increasingly bring to bear what they know about the characters to help them reduce their uncertainty about the content.
6. While this strategy is very useful in the study of fiction, it is adaptable to other content areas as well. During or after reading an appropriate text about the U.S. Civil War battle at Antietam, students might engage in a hot seat activity to examine the perspectives of President Lincoln, President Davis of the Confederate South, Confederate General Robert E. Lee, and Union General George McClellan. In science, students could assume roles of a stem cell researcher, a politician in favor of such research, a politician who opposes the research, and a person who might benefit from stem cell research.

Sitting in the hot seat requires a student to experience a work of literature or historical perspective from a different point of view, thus assisting students to clarify or refine what they know through social interaction. To facilitate implementation of this strategy, consider these modifications:

1. Allow students to work in groups to brainstorm possible questions. Their questions might focus on recalling the story or on speculating about a character's emotions or motivation to act as he or she does.
2. Put students into "expert" character groups so they can share their ideas about characters.
3. Use puppets, character masks, and living murals to liven up the activity.

APPLICATIONS AND EXAMPLES

Ms. Marla Green uses hot seat to help her students understand the characters in the novel *Bud, Not Buddy* (Curtis, 1999).

IN HER OWN WORDS: Marla Green, Kelso School District, Kelso, Washington

The characters that are the focus for this hot seat are: Bud, Toddy Amos, and Mrs. Amos. Students will take on the roles of each character in a small group, then a whole class discussion follows. We will have several completely different views. Through hot seat, students will be able to think about predictions they made about Mrs. Amos' statement: "Lord knows I have been stung by my own people before. But take a good look at me because I am one person who is totally fed up with you and your ilk. I do not have time to put up with the foolishness of those members of our race who do not want to be uplifted." (Curtis, 2002, pp. 14–15) or why Todd beats the heck out of Bud.

REFERENCES

Alatorre-Parks, L. (2001). Aligning student interests with district mandates. *The Journal of Adolescent and Adult Literacy, 44,* 330–332.

Allen, J. (2002). *On the same page: Shared reading beyond the primary grades.* Portland, ME: Stenhouse.

Alvermann, D., & Phelps, S. (2005). *Content reading and literacy: Succeeding in today's diverse classrooms.* Boston: Allyn & Bacon.

Baumann, J. F., Jones, L. A., & Seifert-Kessell, N. (1993). Using think alouds to enhance children's comprehension monitoring abilities. *The Reading Teacher, 47,* 184–193.

Betts, E. A. (1946). *Foundations of reading instruction with emphasis on differentiated guidance.* New York: American Book Company.

Brown, A. L., Campione, J. C., & Day, J. D. (1981). Learning to learn: On training students to learn from texts. *Educational Researcher, 10*(2), 14–21.

Bruer, J. T. (1993). The mind's journey from novice to expert: If we know the route, we can help students negotiate their way. *American Educator, 17*(2), 38–46.

Bryan, J. (1998). K-W-W-L: Questioning the known. *The Reading Teacher, 51,* 618–620.

Burns, A. (2004). Weaving comprehension strategies into double-entry journals. *The California Reader, 37*(4), 20–26.

Carter, C. J. (1997). Why reciprocal teaching? *Educational Leadership, 54*(6), 64–68.

Cazden, C. B. (2001). *Classroom discourse: The language of teaching and learning.* Portsmouth, NH: Heinemann.

Chamot, A. U., & O'Malley, J. M. (1994). *The CALLA handbook: Implementing the cognitive academic language learning approach.* Reading, MA: Addison-Wesley Publishing Company.

Chapman, C., & King, R. (2003). *Differentiated instructional strategies for reading in the content areas.* Thousand Oaks, CA: Corwin Press.

Collins, A., Brown, J. S., & Holum, A. (1991). Cognitive apprenticeship: Making thinking visible. *American Educator, 6*(11), 38–46.

Cunningham, J. W., Cunningham, P. M., & Arthur, S. V. (1981). *Middle and secondary school reading.* New York: Longman.

Curtis, C. P. (1999). *Bud not buddy.* New York. Dell Yearling.

Davidson, M. (1996). *Balto, The dog who saved Nome.* New York: Scholastic.

Davis, D. (2004). *Improving adolescent reading: Findings from research.* Portland, OR: Northwest Regional Educational Laboratory.

Dechant, E. (1991). *Understanding and teaching reading: An interactive model.* Hillsdale, NJ: Lawrence Erlbaum Associates.

Dreher, S. (2003). A novel idea: Reading aloud in a high school English classroom. *English Journal, 93,* 50–53.

Dufflemeyer, F. A. (1994). Effective anticipation guide statements for learning from expository prose. *Journal of Reading, 37,* 452–457.

Dufflemeyer, F. A., & Baum, D. D. (1992). The extended anticipation guide, revisited. *Journal of Reading, 35,* 654–656.

Dufflemeyer, F. A., Baum, D. D., & Merkley, D. J. (1987). Maximizing reader-text confrontation with an extended anticipation guide. *Journal of Reading, 31,* 146–150.

Eby, J. (1998). *Reflective planning, teaching, and evaluation, K–12* (2nd ed.). Upper Saddle River, NJ: Merrill Prentice Hall.

Egan, M. (1999). Reflections on effective use of graphic organizers. *The Journal of Adolescent and Adult Literacy, 42,* 641–645.

Fisher, D., Brozo, W., Frey, N., & Ivey, G. (2007). *Fifty content area strategies for adolescent literacy.* Upper Saddle River, NJ: Pearson, Merrill, Prentice Hall.

Fisher, D., Frey, N., & Williams, D. (2002). Seven literacy strategies that work. *Educational Leadership, 60*(3), 70–73.

Freire, P. (1970). *Pedagogy of the oppressed* (30th anniversary ed.). New York: Continuum.

Fry, E. (2004). Four phonics frequency tables. *The California Reader, 37*(4), 36–43.

Gardner, H. (2006). *Changing minds: The art and science of changing our own and other people's minds.* Boston: Harvard Business School Press.

Graves, B., & Graves, M. (1995). Harness motivation with a scaffolded reading experience. *The California Reader, 29*(1), 28–31.

Haggard, M. R. (1988). Developing critical thinking with the directed reading-thinking activity. *The Reading Teacher, 41,* 526–531.

Harvey, W. F. (1910). August heat. *In Midnight house and other tales.* London: J. M. Dent.

Hayes, D. A. (1989). Helping students GRASP the knack of writing summaries. *Journal of Reading, 33*(2), 96–101.

Hemingway, E. (1952). *The old man and the sea.* London: Jonathan Cape.

Hyde, A. (2006). *Comprehending math: Adapting reading strategies to teach mathematics, K–6.* Portsmouth, NH: Heinemann.

Jacobs, W. W. (1902). The monkey's paw. *Harper's Monthly, 105,* 634–639.

Johnston, F. R. (1993). Improving student response in DR–TAs and DL–TAs. *The Reading Teacher, 46,* 448–449.

MacLachlan, P. (1985). *Sarah, plain and tall.* New York: Harper Collins.

Malcolm X. (1997). Hair. In C. B. Divakaruni (Ed.), *Multitudes: Cross-cultural readings for writers* (pp. 327–329). New York McGraw-Hill.

Mandeville, T. (1994). KWLA: Linking the affective and cognitive domains. *The Reading Teacher, 47,* 679–680.

Marks, M., Pressley, M., Coley, J. D., Craig, S., Gardner, R., DePinto, T., et al. (1993). Three teachers' adaptations of reciprocal teaching in comparison to traditional reciprocal teaching. *The Elementary School Journal, 94,* 267–283.

Ogle, D. (1986). K-W-L: A teaching model that develops active reading of expository text. *The Reading Teacher, 39,* 564–570.

Ogle, D., & Carr, E. (1987). K-W-L plus: A strategy for comprehension and summarization. *Journal of Reading, 30,* 626–631.

Oldfather, P. (1995). Commentary: What's needed to maintain and extend the motivation for literacy in the middle grades. *Journal of Reading, 38,* 420–422.

Palinscar, A. S., & Brown, A. L. (1984). Reciprocal teaching of comprehension-fostering and comprehension-monitoring activities. *Cognition and Instruction, 1,* 117–175.

Parkes, B. (1985). *The three little pigs.* [Rigby big book]. Orlando, FL: Rigby Harcourt.

Postman, N. (1992). *Technolopoly: The surrender of culture to technology.* New York: Vintage Books.

Raphael, T. E. (1984). Teaching learners about sources of information for answering questions. *Journal of Reading, 27,* 303–311.

Raphael, T. E. (1986). Teaching question-answer relationships, revisited. *The Reading Teacher, 39,* 516–520.

Ridgeway, V. G. (1999, May 6). *A view from the other side: A [former] science teacher speaks out.* Presentation at the 44th annual convention of the International Reading Association, San Diego, CA.

Ross, P., & McDaniel, C. (2004). The impact of clinical experience on the reading comprehension instruction of K–12 inservice teachers. *Yearbook of the National Reading Conference, 53,* 321–341.

Ryder, R. J., & Graves, M. F. (2003). *Reading and learning in content areas* (3rd ed.). New York: John Wiley & Sons.

Sagor, R. (2000). *Guiding school improvement with action research.* Alexandria, VA: Association for Supervision and Curriculum Development.

Schmidt, P. (1999). KWLQ: Inquiry and literacy learning in science. *The Reading Teacher, 52,* 789–792.

Sippola, A. E. (1995). K-W-L-S *The Reading Teacher, 48,* 6, 542–543.

Stauffer, R. G. (1969). *Teaching reading as a thinking process.* New York: Harper and Row, Publishers.

Strickland, D. (1998). What's basic in beginning reading? Finding common ground. *Educational Leadership, 55,* 6–10.

Tompkins, G. (2003). *Literacy for the 21st century* (3rd ed.). Upper Saddle River, NJ: Merrill Prentice Hall.

Vacca, R. T., & Vacca, J. L. (2005). *Content area reading: Literacy and learning across the curriculum* (8th ed.). Boston: Pearson Education.

Walker, B. J. (2005). Thinking aloud: Struggling readers often require more than a model. *The Reading Teacher, 58,* 688–692.

Wilhelm, J. D. (1999). Think-alouds boost reading comprehension. *Instructor, 111*(4), 26–28.

Wilhelm, J. D. (2001). Getting kids into the reading game: You gotta know the rules. *Voices from the Middle, 8*(4), 25–36.

IV

Using Predictions to Increase Precision Teaching

As we have noted, teaching well requires a series of complex interactions between teachers and students. Of course students also learn from interactions with other students, their family members, and the world around them. However, this book focuses on the interactions that teachers plan to have with their students. We believe that these interactions should result in the internalization of strategies such that they become habits.

For us, the key to student learning centers on habit building. As teachers, we have to develop, facilitate, foster, coach, or (insert the verb of your choice) students as they become increasingly proficient at thinking about and understanding texts. Doing so requires a great deal of precision as Fullan, Hill, and Crévola (2006) point out. Teaching with precision, compared with teaching from a script (prescriptive), requires that teachers understand their content standards, understand their students' needs and interests, and can use instructional routines to provide students with feedback such that they become increasingly confident and competent.

✺ KNOWING STUDENTS

There are several ways to get to know students, the most obvious of which is kid watching. Other great ways to get to know students include interest inventories and surveys. Of course, formal assessments of reading comprehension and evaluations of writing samples provide additional ways of getting to know students.

Kid Watching

As Goodman (1985) pointed out, teachers can learn a great deal about their students from purposeful observations. Of course, you can't watch every student every minute. Instead, we recommend that you focus on specific students each day and ask yourself how the focus student reacts to instruction. Our colleague, Principal Emily Schell, developed a tool for teachers to help one another kid watch. In partners, teachers can use the form in Figure IV.1 to engage in conversations about the ways in which students respond to instruction.

The practice of helping a peer to kid watch also improves your own practice. As Jessica Torres noted, "I visit Ms. Allen every week and helped her kid watch. We wanted to see how specific students were responding to teacher modeling. I know that Ms. Allen found it helpful, but it really helped me focus on students in my own classroom. I got so much better at kid watching and doing something about what I saw."

And this is the key: doing something about what you see. Lots of us have watched kids but did not know what to do about what we saw. Precision requires both a system of learning about students AND a system for providing students feedback. As you might have predicted, we'll discuss feedback a bit later in this chapter. For now, we'll stay focused on knowing students.

Interest Inventory

Another way to get to know students is through the use of an interest inventory. Interest inventories help you get to know students and make connections with the things that are important to them. These tools become especially important when students are not engaged or are not progressing. As we were reminded by Jeff Blackstone, "I had this student who just couldn't get it. She really struggled with predicting. I realized that she just didn't care about the texts we were reading. I reviewed her interest inventory and was reminded that she really liked people and that she wanted to read biographies. I got a couple of short, picture book biographies and started talking with her about prediction strategies using the lives of people in the books. She got it and she cared about it. I guess I was reminded that learning happens when students are interested. She learned to make much more sophisticated predictions, and engage with texts, when they were personally meaningful." Figure IV.2 contains a sample interest inventory.

Metacomprehension Strategy Index

The appendix of this chapter contains the Metacomprehension Strategy Index (Schmitt, 1990), a tool useful in determining which strategies students use and which they confuse. We use this instrument to determine which strategies students have mastered and which require additional instruction and practice. The goal is to ensure that these instructional strategies become automatic cognitive processes. Without an assessment to determine which strategies are being incorporated into students' habits and which are not, precision teaching is not possible.

Assessments

We won't take much time here to focus on assessments, other than to remind you that formal reading and writing assessments provide information that is critical for teaching. Assessments allow teachers to plan and differentiate instruction. Without assessments, we are forced to teach to the middle and not at all with precision.

For example, Aida Allen assessed her students' writing to determine the type of instruction they needed (Fisher & Frey, 2007). She looked for specific components of writing development, such as sentence fluency, word choice, and average number of errors per sentence, to plan her instruction.

Figure IV.1   Observation Tool

OBSERVATIONS OF STUDENTS AT WORK

The host teacher will use this during the pre-observation meeting to explain the focus of the lesson. Attached will be a lesson plan for the visiting teacher to understand and follow the lesson. The lesson plan will identify the standard(s), goals and objectives, strategy/strategies for the learning activity, and materials.

FOCUS Strategy:		
FOCUS Student(s):		
What the teacher says/does:	**How the students respond:**	**Questions I have:**

Source: Emily Schell, 2007. Used with permission.

Figure IV.2   Sample Interest Inventory

Name:_____	**Date:**_____

   1. Who is a good reader you know?

   2. What makes him or her a good reader?

   3. If your friends could only say one word about you, what would it be?

   4. Do you prefer to be inside or outside?

   5. What is the best way to spend your free time?

   6. When you go to a library or bookstore, what type of books do you look for?

   7. Who is your favorite author?

   8. What is your all-time favorite book?

   9. What is your favorite type of book to read?

10. What was the last book you read?

11. Where is your favorite place to read?

12. Think about science; what's your favorite topic?

13. Think about social studies; what's your favorite topic?

14. Do you like art, music, or physical education? What would you like to learn more about in these areas?

You might be wondering how an example about writing instruction fits in a book about predicting. It's simple really. Writing is thinking. We all think as we write. What we're trying to do in our focus on predicting is to facilitate thinking. We see evidence of this thinking in student's writing. As they become more sophisticated thinkers, students become more sophisticated writers. The reverse is also true. If we help students become better writers, we're also helping them become better thinkers.

Of course there are all kinds of assessments that are helpful for teachers as they plan instruction. Some useful assessment books include:

- Barone, D. M., & Taylor, J. M. (2006). *The practical guide to classroom literacy assessment.* Thousand Oaks, CA: Corwin.

- Fisher, D., & Frey, N. (2007). *Checking for understanding: Formative assessments for your classroom.* Alexandria, VA: Association for Supervision and Curriculum Development.

- Paratore, J. R., & McCormack, R. L. (Eds.). (2007). New York: Guilford.

❧ PROFILES IN COMPREHENSION

In addition to the information you can obtain about students from observations, surveys, and assessments, understanding comprehension profiles can improve precision teaching. Applegate, Quinn, and Applegate (2006), based on their analysis of thousands of student responses, identified eight types of comprehenders: literalists, fuzzy thinkers, left fielders, quiz contestants, politicians, dodgers, authors, and minimalists. As is evident in

Figure IV.3, there are significant differences in these types of comprehenders. As we read their work, we realized that we have had each and every one of these types of comprehenders in our classrooms.

Based on the work of Applegate, Quinn, and Applegate (2006), we have identified specific cognitive strategies and instructional routines useful in addressing each type of comprehender. Again, this is about precision. Understanding students and how they think helps teachers plan instruction that works. What might work for a literalist might not work for a politician.

As you know from reading this book, we believe that matching students with specific instruction is critical for improving achievement. Understanding these differences allows you an opportunity to plan instruction and feedback, all with the goal of causing thinking. In the next section, we'll link the comprehension profiles with feedback systems, thereby closing the instructional circle.

✿ FEEDBACK

Feedback is easy to define: It is interaction between two individuals designed to increase learning. Often, feedback provides just the right information at just the right time to transform a competent performance into an exemplary one. Or it may be the critical explanation through use of analogy that a teacher makes for a student struggling with a challenge that turns a difficult task into a new conceptualization. Effective predictions are a means of thinking about a topic, and the precision with which students make predictions can be scaffolded through effective feedback. The instructional routines you have explored in this book also provide an excellent venue for increasing the type and quality of feedback you provide to your students. Hattie and Timperley (2007) proposed a model of feedback that includes the idea that effective feedback helps students to know where they are going in terms of goals (called feed up), how they are doing on the current learning task (called feed back), and where they might go next (called feed forward). Notice how the teachers use these three qualities of feedback in the following examples.

Using Feed Up to Establish Goals

John scanned the science textbook over and over, his eyes moving back and forth, his index finger tracing lines through the columns looking for the key words he felt he needed. He kept looking over the text until his hand slowly went up as he realized that the information he needed wasn't in the text and he didn't know what to do. "Mr. Carver, the question asks what would happen after a fire in an old growth forest, but I can't find the answer anywhere in this stupid chapter." Mr. Carver knew that John expected the answer to be stated directly in the text, the profile of the literalist comprehender. The easiest thing would just be to tell John what he needed to know, but Mr. Carver wanted John to learn to make inferences and he had recently taught his class to use Question Answer Relationships (QAR) (Rafael, 1984, 1986).

With just a few questions, Mr. Carver reminded John that he read about old growth forests. John flipped to the page and reviewed the text. Then Mr. Carver asked John if he had read about the effects of the fire in Yellowstone in 1988, by which time John had figured it out. But Mr. Carver wasn't done yet; John had something else to learn. John was used to looking for answers and assumed that they were all literally in the words on the pages. Referring to the QAR chart on the wall beside them, Mr. Carver asked John which

Figure IV.3 Profiles, Cognitive Strategies, and Instructional Routines

Profile	Description	Cognitive Strategies	Instructional Routines
1. Literalists	Look for all answers to all types of questions to be stated in the text.	Accessing background and prior knowledge, making inferences, making connections, making and asking for clarifications.	KWL, QAR, DR-TA, reciprocal teaching
2. Fuzzy Thinkers	Provide vague, ambiguous, or trite responses.	Visualizing, summarizing, attending to text features, generating questions, making and asking for clarifications.	Reciprocal teaching, graphic organizers, anticipation guides
3. Left Fielders	Generate unpredictable ideas that seem to have no real connection to the text.	Summarizing, making inferences.	Metacognitive double-entry journals, guided reading and summarizing procedure
4. Quiz Contestants	Provide answers that are logically correct but disconnected from the text.	Making textually implicit inferences, generating questions.	QAR, reciprocal teaching, metacognitive double-entry journals
5. Politicians	Use slogans or platitudes that sound meaningful but are not text connected.	Generating and responding to questions.	QAR, anticipation guides, cliffhanger
6. Dodgers	Change the question and then respond to the new one.	Responding to questions, making textually-implicit inferences, attending to text features.	QAR, hot seat
7. Authors	Create their own story lines and story details.	Visualizing, summarizing, attending to literary devices.	QAR, guided reading and summarizing procedure, KWL
8. Minimalists	Provide no elaboration of responses, resulting from lack of confidence or fear of failure.	Summarizing, visualizing, making inferences, accessing background and prior knowledge.	Think aloud, hot seat, reciprocal teaching

Adapted from Applegate, M. D., Quinn, K. B., & Applegate, A. J. (2006). Profiles in comprehension. *The Reading Teacher, 60,* 48–57.

question type from the chart the question about old growth fires had been. It was a "think and search" question, of course, and because Mr. Carver paid attention to the cognitive strategies John was relying upon, he could provide feedback that would help John with the present problem about forest fires and perform better next time he was stuck looking for something that was literally not there.

In this example, Mr. Carver provided feed up to John to help him know how he was doing in terms of the goal of making inferences. He also provided feedback that let John know where he could adjust his understanding of the text and the cognitive strategies he should employ.

Feed Back In the Classroom

In small group discussion, the students had just read about the Irish potato famine. Their task, outlined by the teacher, was to determine what might have happened if the blight had been contained. Just as Dinah asked for ideas, Mike blurted out, "There must be a lot of Irish people in Idaho because they grow so many potatoes there." Dinah was a little flustered, but quickly recovered; students can provide good feed back for one another, too. She knew that Mike had jumped for the buzzer, like a contestant on a quiz show eager to say something—anything—first. Remembering the reciprocal teaching strategies they often uses in class, she said, "Hmmm, Mike, I don't think there was anything about Idaho in the book, but who can summarize the reading to help us remember for sure?" Precision teaching earlier helped Dinah's group learn from the reading, employ sophisticated cognitive strategies, and provide useful feedback to each other in order to make their group work more productive.

Dinah, modeling her responses on those of her teacher, helped Mike by providing feedback on how he was doing by employing the summarize strategy. In doing so, she focused the discussion by sending the students in her group back to the text for the information they needed to make successful predictions.

Integrating Feed Forward in Instruction

> We selected for our victim the only child of a prominent citizen named Ebenezer Dorset. The father was respectable and tight, a mortgage fancier and a stern, upright collection-plate passer and forecloser. The kid was a boy of ten, with basrelief freckles, and hair the color of the cover of the magazine you buy at the news-stand when you want to catch a train. Bill and me figured that Ebenezer would melt down for a ransom of two thousand dollars to a cent. But wait till I tell you. (Henry, 1910/1994, p. 425)

After the students finish reading the page in the short story, "The Ransom of Red Chief," the teacher asks for predictions. In this story, the narrator and his accomplice plan to kidnap the son of a prominent citizen in a small town in Alabama, but nothing goes according to their plan. Sam tells the small group of students that kidnapping is "just wrong" but Mrs. Lewis wants more than a politician's slogan. So, after students summarize what they know of the story, so far, she asks them for predictions again. In the cliffhanger, students refer to important elements of the introduction to this story. The narrator of the story has just dropped a clue that something did not go according to the kidnapping plan he's laid out. John learned from his science teacher to make inferences by looking for information in different places in the text and putting it together; he applies the information now. "Mrs. Lewis, I read that the town is on a flat place but called Summit. Also, the first sentence of the story starts out with, 'It looked like a good thing; but wait till I tell you.' So I'm thinking that nothing in this story will follow the bad guys' plans. And, isn't an 'apparition' a ghost? Bill called their idea a 'temporary mental apparition.' That doesn't make any sense." Mrs. Lewis notes that John has, indeed, learned to make his own predictions based on his reading of the story. Her feedback this time is just to note that he has used an inference to make a prediction, asked a question about vocabulary use, and used that information to make another prediction.

As the story unfolds and the students' discussion unfolds with it, Mrs. Lewis often names the cognitive strategies the students are using while she employs an instructional routine to promote their good thinking about the story, overcoming the obstacles that still pop up from the comprehender profiles from time to time. Mrs. Lewis feeds forward the strategies the students have learned so that they are increasingly able to use them again in the future. By naming the type of thinking displayed, the students know what they have done well (feed back) and that they can successfully do so again (feed forward).

❧ CONCLUSION

Successfully choosing instructional routines to encourage cognitive strategies amongst your students is something teachers do almost automatically. By thinking about the cognitive demands of specific texts, knowing which are needed by using models like the comprehender profiles, and applying instructional routines, teachers can increase the precision with which they approach predicting and consequently comprehension. This book provides an approach for putting these elements together, and you may find yourself using these ideas as a basis for discussion with your colleagues, as well. Through such professional discussions, we can scaffold our own understanding of our students and make increasingly accurate predictions about what students need in order to be thoughtful and precise when they read.

REFERENCES

Applegate, M. D., Quinn, K. B., & Applegate, A. J. (2006). Profiles in comprehension. *The Reading Teacher, 60,* 48–57.

Fisher, D., & Frey, N. (2007). *Scaffolding writing instruction: Teaching with a gradual-release framework*. New York: Scholastic.

Fullan, M., Hill, P., & Crévola, C. (2006). *Breakthrough*. Thousand Oaks, CA: Corwin.

Goodman, Y. (1985). Kid watching: Observing children in the classroom. In A. Jaggar & M. T. Smith-Burke (Eds.), *Observing the language learner* (pp. 9–18). Newark, DE: International Reading Association and the National Council of Teachers of English.

Hattie, J., & Timperley, H. (2007). The power of feedback. *Review of Educational Research, 77,* 81–112.

Henry, O. (1910/1994). The ransom of Red Chief. *O. Henry: Selected stories*. New York: Book-of-the-Month Club.

Raphael, T. E . (1984). Teaching learners about sources of information for answering questions. *Journal of Reading, 27,* 303–311.

Raphael, T. E. (1986). Teaching question-answer relationships, revisited, *The Reading Teacher, 39,* 516–520.

Schmitt, M. C. (1990). A questionnaire to measure children's awareness of strategic reading processes. *The Reading Teacher, 43,* 454–461.

Appendix

Metacomprehension Strategy Index

Name:_____   Date:_____

Metacomprehension Strategy Index

Directions: Think about what kinds of things you can do to help you understand a story better before, during, and after you read it. Read each of the lists of four statements and decide which one of them would help you the most. Circle the letter of the statement you choose.

I. In each set of four, choose the one statement which tells a good thing to do to help you understand a story better *before* you read it.

1. Before I begin reading, it's a good idea to:
   A. See how many pages are in the story.
   B. Look up all of the big words in the dictionary.
   C. Make some guesses about what I think will happen in the story.
   D. Think about what has happened so far in the story.

2. Before I begin reading, it's a good idea to:
   A. Look at the pictures to see what the story is about.
   B. Decide how long it will take me to read the story.
   C. Sound out the words I don't know.
   D. Check to see if the story is making sense.

3. Before I begin reading, it's a good idea to:
   A. Ask someone to read the story to me.
   B. Read the title to see what the story is about.
   C. Check to see if most of the words have long or short vowels in them.
   D. Check to see if the pictures are in order and make sense.

4. Before I begin reading, it's a good idea to:
   A. Check to see that no pages are missing.
   B. Make a list of words I'm not sure about.
   C. Use the title and pictures to help me make guesses about what will happen in the story.
   D. Read the last sentence so I will know how the story ends.

5. Before I begin reading, it's a good idea to:
   A. Decide on why I am going to read the story.
   B. Use the difficult words to help me make guesses about what will happen in the story.
   C. Reread some parts to see if I can figure out what is happening if things aren't making sense.
   D. Ask for help with the difficult words.

6. Before I begin reading, it's a good idea to:
   A. Retail all of the main points that have happened so far.
   B. Ask myself questions that I would like to have answered in the story.
   C. Think about the meaning of the words, which have more than one meaning.
   D. Look through the story to find all of the words with three or more syllables.

7. Before I begin reading, it's a good idea to:
   A. Check to see if I have read this story before.
   B. Use my questions and guesses as a reason for reading the story.
   C. Make sure I can pronounce all of the words before I start.
   D. Think of a better title for the story.

8. Before I begin reading, it's a good idea to:
   A. Think of what I already know about the things see in the pictures.
   B. See how many pages are in the story.
   C. Choose the best part of the story to read again.
   D. Read the story aloud to someone.

9. Before I begin reading, it's a good idea to:
   A. Practice reading the story out loud.
   B. Retail all of the main points to make sure I can remember the story.
   C. Think of what the people in the story might be like.
   D. Decide if I have enough time to read the story.

10. Before I begin reading, it's a good idea to:
    A. Check to see if I am understanding the story so far.
    B. Check to see if the words have more than one meaning.
    C. Think about where the story might be taking place.
    D. List all of the important details.

II. In each set of four, choose the one statement which tells a good thing to do to help you understand a story better *while* you are reading it.

11. While I am reading, it's a good idea to:
    A. Read the story very slowly so that I will not miss any important parts.
    B. Read the title to see what the story is about.
    C. Check to see if the pictures have anything missing.
    D. Check to see if the story is making sense by seeing if I can tell what's happened so far.

12. While I am reading, it's good idea to:
    A. Stop to retail the main points to see if I am understanding what has happened so far.
    B. Read the story quickly so that I can find out what happened.
    C. Read only the beginning and the end of the story to find out what it is about.
    D. Skip the parts that are too difficult for me.

13. While I am reading, it's a good idea to:
    A. Look all of the big words up in the dictionary.
    B. Put the book away and find another one if things aren't making sense.
    C. Keep thinking about the title and the pictures to help me decide what is going to happen next.
    D. Keep track of how many pages I have left to read.

14. While I am reading, it's a good idea to:
    A. Keep track of how long it is taking me to read the story.
    B. Check to see if I can answer any of the questions I asked before I started reading.
    C. Read the title to see what the story is going to be about.
    D. Add the missing details to the pictures.

15. While I am reading, it's good idea to:
    A. Have someone read the story aloud to me.
    B. Keep track of how many pages I have read.
    C. List the story's main character.
    D. Check to see if my guesses are right or wrong.

16. While I am reading, it's a good idea to:
    A. Check to see that the characters are real.
    B. Make a lot of guesses about what is going to happen next.
    C. Not look at the pictures because they might confuse me.
    D. Read the story aloud to someone.

17. While I am reading, it's a good idea to:
    A. Try to answer the questions I asked myself.
    B. Try not to confuse what I already know with what I am reading about.
    C. Read the story silently.
    D. Check to see if I am saying the new vocabulary words correctly.

18. While I am reading, it's a good idea to:
    A. Try to see if my guesses are going to be right or wrong.
    B. Reread to be sure I haven't missed any of the words.
    C. Decide on why I am reading the story.
    D. List what happened first, second, third, and so on.

19. While I am reading, it's a good idea to:
    A. See if I can recognize the new vocabulary words.
    B. Be careful not to skip any parts of the story.
    C. Check to see how many of the words I already know.
    D. Keep thinking of what I already know about the things and ideas in the story to help me decide what is going to happen.

20. While I am reading, it's a good idea to:
    A. Reread some parts or read ahead to see if I can figure out what is happening if things aren't making sense.
    B. Take my time reading so that I can be sure I understand what is happening.
    C. Change the ending so that it makes sense.
    D. Check to see if there are enough pictures to help make the story ideas clear.

III. In each set of four, choose the one statement which tells a good thing to do to help you understand a story better *after* you have read it.

21. After I've read a story, it's good idea to:
    A. Count how many pages I read with no mistakes.
    B. Check to see if there were enough pictures to go with the story to make it interesting.
    C. Check to see if I met my purpose for reading the story.
    D. Underline the causes and effects.

22. After I've read a story, it's a good idea to:
    A. Underline the main idea.
    B. Retell the main points of the whole story so that I can check to see if I understood it.
    C. Read the story again to be sure I said all of the words right.
    D. Practice reading the story aloud.

23. After I've read a story, it's a good idea to:
    A. Read the title and look over the story to see what it is about.
    B. Check to see if I skipped any of the vocabulary words.
    C. Think about what made me make good or bad predictions.
    D. Make a guess about what will happen next in the story.

24. After I've read a story, it's a good idea to:
    A. Look up all of the big words in the dictionary.
    B. Read the best parts aloud.
    C. Have someone read the story aloud to me.
    D. Think about how the story was like things I already knew about before I started reading.

25. After I've read a story, it's a good idea to:
    A. Think about how I would have acted if I were the main character in the story.
    B. Practice reading the story silently for practice of good reading.
    C. Look over the story title and picture to see what will happen.
    D. Make a list of the things I understood the most.

Source: Schmitt, M. C. (March 1990). A questionnaire to measure children's awareness of strategic reading processes. *The Reading Teacher, 43,* 454–461.

Intrepeting Results of the Metacomprehension Strategy Index

The MSI (Schmitt, 1990) is a measure of a student's use of strategies with narrative text. It may be read to the student, or administered silently. The wording of the items can be substituted to reflect expository text. For example, you can replace the wording of #2 to read,

Before I begin reading, it's a good idea to:
A. Look at the pictures to see what the story is about.
B. Decide how long it will take me to read the story.
C. Sound out the words I don't know.
D. Check to see if the story is making sense.

Answer Key: The following item analysis is organized to more fully describe the types of matacomprehension strategies tested.

1. C	6. B	11. D	16. B	21. C
2. A	7. B	12. A	17. A	22. B
3. B	8. A	13. C	18. A	23. C
4. C	9. C	14. B	19. D	24. D
5. A	10. C	15. D	20. A	25. A

Interpreting: These answers represent the best answers; items may include strategies that are somewhat useful but not as efficient for the situation described.

Strategies	Items
Predicting and Verifying Predicting and verifying the content of a story promotes active comprehension by giving readers a purpose to read (i.e., to verify predictions). Evaluating predictions and generating new ones as necessary enhances the constructive nature of the reading process.	1, 4, 13, 15, 16, 18, 23
Previewing Previewing the text facilitates comprehension by activating background knowledge and providing information for making predictions.	2, 3
Purpose Setting Reading with a purpose promotes active, strategic reading.	5, 7, 21
Self-questioning Generating questions to be answered promotes active comprehension by giving readers a purpose for reading (i.e., to answer the questions).	6, 14, 17
Drawing from Background Knowledge Activating and incorporating information from background knowledge contributes to comprehension by helping readers make inferences and generate predictions	8, 9, 10, 19, 24, 25
Summarizing and Applying fix-up Strategies Summarizing the content at various points in the story serves as a form of comprehension monitoring. Rereading or suspending judgment and reading on when comprehension breaks down represents strategic reading.	11, 12, 20, 22

Source: Adapted from Schmitt, M.C. (1900). A questionnaire to measure children's awareness of strategic reading processes. *The Reading Teacher, 43,* 454–461. Used with permission.